W9-BRP-208

AP® EUROPEAN HISTORY
CRASH COURSE®

By Larry Krieger

Research & Education Association
Visit our website at: www.rea.com

Research & Education Association
61 Ethel Road West
Piscataway, New Jersey 08854
E-mail: info@rea.com

AP® EUROPEAN HISTORY CRASH COURSE®

Published 2015

Printed in the United States of America

Library of Congress Control Number 2009933695

ISBN-13: 978-0-7386-0661-3
ISBN-10: 0-7386-0661-8

AP EUROPEAN HISTORY CRASH COURSE
TABLE OF CONTENTS

PART III:

Key Themes and Facts

PART IV:

Test-Taking Strategies

Online Practice Exam................. *www.rea.com/studycenter*

ABOUT THIS BOOK

REA's *AP European History Crash Course* is the first book of its kind for the last-minute studier or any AP student who wants a quick refresher on the course. The *Crash Course* is based upon a careful analysis of the AP European History Course Description outline and actual AP test questions.

Written by an expert who has studied the AP European History (APEURO) exam content for 20 years, our easy-to-read format gives students a crash course in the major ideas and events in European history. The targeted review chapters prepare students for the exam by focusing on the important topics tested on the AP European History exam.

Unlike other test preps, REA's *AP European History Crash Course* gives you a review specifically focused on what you really need to study in order to ace the exam. The review chapters offer you a concise way to learn all the important facts, terms, and key themes before the exam.

The introduction discusses the keys for success and shows you strategies to help you build your overall point score. It also gives you a list of Key Terms that you absolutely, positively have to know. Parts Two and Three are composed of chapters offering chronological and thematic reviews. Each chapter presents the essential information you need to know about European History.

Part Four focuses exclusively on the format of the AP European History exam. Each chapter in this section explains specific strategies for the multiple-choice questions, the document-based question and the free-response essays.

No matter how or when you prepare for the AP European History exam, REA's *Crash Course* will show you how to study efficiently and strategically, so you can boost your score!

To check your test readiness for the AP European History exam, either before or after studying this *Crash Course*, take REA's **FREE online practice exam**. To access your practice exam, visit the online REA Study Center at *www.rea.com/studycenter* and follow the on-screen instructions. This true-to-format test features automatic scoring, detailed explanations of all answers, and diagnostic score reporting that will help you identify your strengths and weaknesses so you'll be ready on exam day!

Good luck on your AP European History exam!

ABOUT OUR AUTHOR

Larry Krieger earned his B.A. and M.A.T. from the University of North Carolina at Chapel Hill and his M.A. from Wake Forest University. In a career spanning more than 35 years, Mr. Krieger has taught a variety of AP subjects including American History, World History, European History, American Government, and Art History. His popular courses were renowned for their energetic presentations, commitment to scholarship, and helping students achieve high AP exam scores. All of Mr. Krieger's students scored above a 3, with most students scoring a 4 or a 5. In 2004 and 2005, the College Board recognized Mr. Krieger as one of the nation's foremost AP teachers.

Mr. Krieger's success has extended far beyond the classroom. He conducts SAT and AP workshops around the country, and has spoken at numerous Social Studies conferences. In addition, he is the author of several widely used American History and World History textbooks, as well as REA's *Crash Course* test preps for European History, U.S. History, U.S. Government & Politics, and Psychology.

ACKNOWLEDGMENTS

In addition to our author, we would like to thank Larry B. Kling, Vice President, Editorial, for his overall guidance, which brought this publication to completion; Pam Weston, Vice President, Publishing, for setting the quality standards for production integrity and managing the publication to completion; Diane Goldschmidt, Senior Editor, for editorial project management; Alice Leonard, Senior Editor, for preflight editorial review; and Rachel DiMatteo, Graphic Artist, for page design.

We would also like to extend special thanks to Caroline Duffy for copyediting, Ellen Gong for proofreading, and Kathy Caratozzolo of Caragraphics for typesetting this edition.

Eight Keys for Success on the AP European History Exam

AP European History textbooks are very thick and contain thousands of names, dates, places, and events. If all of these facts had an equal chance of appearing on your Advanced Placement European History (APEURO) exam, studying would be a nightmare. Where would you begin? What would you emphasize? Is there any information you can safely omit? Or must you study everything?

Fortunately, preparing for the APEURO exam does not have to be a nightmare. By studying efficiently and strategically, you can score a 4 or a 5 on the exam. This book will help you understand and use the following eight keys for success:

1. Understanding the APEURO Scale

Many students believe they must make close to a perfect score to receive a 5. Nothing could be further from the truth. Each APEURO exam contains a total of 180 points – 90 from the multiple-choice and 90 from the free-response questions. Here is the score range from the 2004 Released Exam:

Score Range	AP Grade	Minimum Percent Right
126–180	5	70 percent
106–125	4	58 percent
77–105	3	42 percent
60–76	2	33 percent
0–59	1	0–32 percent

This chart is not a misprint. As is clearly shown, you can achieve a 5 by correctly answering just 70 percent of the questions and a 4 by correctly answering just 58 percent of the questions!

2. Understanding the APEURO Topical Themes

Many students believe that members of the APEURO exam development committee have the freedom to write any question they wish. This widespread belief is not true. APEURO test writers follow an outline devoted to the following three themes:

- Intellectual and Cultural History

- Political and Diplomatic History

- Social and Economic History

The full topical outline is freely available. You can see it in the *AP European History Course Description Booklet*.

The APEURO topical outline is short but very important. According to the Course Description Booklet, "approximately one-third of the questions focus on cultural and intellectual themes, one-third on political and diplomatic themes, and one-third on social and economic themes." This distribution of questions explains why there are so many questions on key intellectual figures, major diplomatic agreements, and economic policies. It also explains why it is a waste of time to study battles, generals, and specific dates.

3. Understanding the Importance of Released Exams

The College Board has released APEURO exams for the years 1984, 1988, 1994, 1999, and 2004. In addition, they provided an online exam for all teachers who participated in the AP course audit. Taken together, these six exams contain 520 multiple-choice questions. This book is based upon a careful analysis of these released questions as well as European history questions on released SAT Subject Tests in World History. These questions can be used to understand the priorities and patterns of the APEURO test writers. It is important to understand that the test writers' top priority is to write an exam that is a valid and reliable measure of a defined body of knowledge. As a result, test questions cluster around very predictable and often-repeated topics. For example, Karl Marx, the Edict of Nantes, and mercantilism have appeared on almost every test. In contrast, you won't find any questions on the Battle of Waterloo or specific inventions that contributed to the growth of the cotton textile industry in England.

4. Understanding the Importance of Key Topics

A content analysis of multiple-choice questions on the 2004 and 1999 released exams reveals important clusters of questions on these four topics:

Topic	2004 Exam	1999 Exam
Key Terms	12 questions	15 questions
Key Treaties and Agreements	7 questions	8 questions
Key Intellectual Figures	9 questions	11 questions
Russian History	6 questions	7 questions

These four topics generated 34 multiple-choice questions on the 2004 exam and 41 multiple-choice questions on the 1999 exam. Since each multiple-choice question is worth 1.125 points, these four topics were worth 38.25 points on the 2004 exam and 46.12 points on the 1999 exam. Remember, you only need a minimum of 126 points to earn a 5 and 106 points to earn a 4. These four topics and the multiple-choice questions they generated would put you well on your way toward earning a 4 or a 5.

5. Understanding the Overlap Between the Multiple-Choice Questions and the Free-Response Questions

Both the multiple-choice questions and the free-response questions are taken from the topical outline in the *Course Description Booklet*. As a result, studying for the multiple-choice questions is tantamount to studying for the free-response questions. Most students fail to grasp the significance of this point. Since the multiple-choice questions are highly predictable, so are the free-response questions. The two types of questions are, in fact, highly related, since they both come from the same topical outline.

6. Understanding How to Prepare for the Free-Response Questions

The Free-Response section of your exam begins with a mandatory Document-Based Essay Question (DBQ) worth 40.5 points. Chapter 27 in this book provides you with detailed strategies for answering the DBQ. You then have two sets of three free-response thematic essay questions. You must answer one question from each set. Each free-response essay is worth 24.75 points for a total of 49.5 points. Chapter 28 provides you with detailed strategies for answering the thematic essay questions.

Many of the *Crash Course* chapters in this book have a special feature called "Making Comparisons." This feature is designed to provide you with in-depth discussions of key topics asked on thematic essays. The Making Comparisons feature will help you develop the analytical skill of noting similarities and differences between key concepts, leaders, events, and trends.

7. **Understanding How to Use Your *Crash Course* to Build a Winning Coalition of Points**

This *Crash Course* book is based on a careful analysis of the *Course Description* topical outline and the released questions. Chapter 2 contains key terms that you absolutely, positively have to know. Chapters 3–22 provide you with a detailed chronological review of European history. And finally, Chapters 23–25 provide you with key facts about themes that regularly appear on each exam.

If you have the time, review the entire book. This is desirable, but not mandatory. The chapters can be studied in any order. Each chapter provides you with a digest of key information that is repeatedly tested. Battles, inventions, rulers, and political events that have never been asked about have been omitted. Unlike most review books, the digests are not meant to be exhaustive. Instead, they are meant to focus your attention on the vital material you must study.

Focus your attention on building a coalition of topics that will generate the points you need to score a 4 or a 5. Key terms, diplomatic agreements, intellectual leaders and events in Russian history are the essential building blocks of any successful coalition.

Although they are important, these topics are just the beginning. The Renaissance, Reformation, French Revolution, women's history, and the Cold War are very focused topics that typically generate three to five questions each.

Many students find it useful to use the chronological chapters to concentrate on a specific period of time. The multiple-choice questions are distributed as follows:

High Renaissance to the French Revolution	50 percent or 40 questions
Nineteenth Century	25 percent or 20 questions
Twentieth Century	25 percent or 20 questions

As you devise your chronological strategy, keep in mind that there are no questions before 1450. Very few questions cover the period from the fall of the Soviet Union in 1991 to the present.

8. **Using College Board and REA Materials to Supplement Your** *Crash Course*

This *Crash Course* contains everything you need to know to score a 4 or a 5 on your exam. You should, however, supplement it with other materials designed specifically for studying AP European History. Visit the College Board's AP Central website for essay questions and sample responses. In addition, REA's *AP European History All Access* Book + Web + Mobile study system further enhances your exam preparation by offering a comprehensive review book plus a suite of online assessments (chapter quizzes, mini-tests, a full-length practice test, and e-flashcards) all designed to pinpoint your strengths and weaknesses and help focus your study for the exam.

Key Terms

 I. **EUROPE IN TRANSITION, 1450–1650**

1. HUMANISM

The scholarly interest in the study of the classical texts, values, and styles of Greece and Rome. Humanism contributed to the promotion of a liberal arts education based on the study of the classics, rhetoric, and history.

2. CHRISTIAN HUMANISM

A branch of humanism associated with northern Europe. Like their Italian counterparts, the Christian humanists closely studied classical texts. However, they also sought to give humanism a specifically Christian content. Christian humanists like Desiderius Erasmus were committed to religious piety and institutional reform.

3. VERNACULAR

The everyday language of a region or country. Miguel de Cervantes, Geoffrey Chaucer, Dante, and Martin Luther all encouraged the development of their national languages by writing in the vernacular. Desiderius Erasmus, however, continued to write in Latin.

4. NEW MONARCHS

European monarchs who created professional armies and a more centralized administrative bureaucracy. The new monarchs also negotiated a new relationship with the Catholic Church. Key new monarchs include Charles VII, Louis XI, Henry VII, and Ferdinand and Isabella.

5. TAILLE

A direct tax on the French peasantry. The taille was one of the most important sources of income for French monarchs until the French Revolution.

6. RECONQUISTA

The centuries-long Christian "reconquest" of Spain from the Muslims. The Reconquista culminated in 1492 with the conquest of the last Muslim stronghold, Granada.

7. INDULGENCE

A certificate granted by the pope in return for the payment of a fee to the church. The certificate stated that the soul of the dead relative or friend of the purchaser would have his time in purgatory reduced by many years or cancelled altogether.

8. ANABAPTIST

Protestants who insisted that only adult baptism conformed to Scripture. Protestant and Catholic leaders condemned Anabaptists for advocating the complete separation of church and state.

9. PREDESTINATION

Doctrine espoused by John Calvin that God has known since the beginning of time who will be saved and who will be damned. Calvin declared that "by an eternal and immutable counsel, God has once and for all determined, both whom he would admit to salvation, and whom he would condemn to destruction."

10. HUGUENOTS

French Protestants who followed the teachings of John Calvin

11. POLITIQUES

Rulers who put political necessities above personal beliefs. For example, both Henry IV of France and Elizabeth I of England subordinated theological controversies in order to achieve political unity.

12. COLUMBIAN EXCHANGE

The interchange of plants, animals, diseases, and human populations between the Old World and the New World

13. MERCANTILISM

Economic philosophy calling for close government regulation of the economy. Mercantilist theory emphasized building a strong, self-sufficient economy by maximizing exports and limiting imports. Mercantilists supported the acquisition of colonies as sources of raw materials and markets for finished goods. This favorable balance of trade would enable a country to accumulate reserves of gold and silver.

14. PUTTING-OUT SYSTEM

A preindustrial manufacturing system in which an entrepreneur would bring materials to rural people who worked on them in their own homes. For example, watch manufacturers in Swiss towns employed villagers to make parts for their products. The system enabled entrepreneurs to avoid restrictive guild regulations.

15. JOINT-STOCK COMPANY

A business arrangement in which many investors raise money for a venture too large for any of them to undertake alone. They share the profits in proportion to the amount they invest. English entrepreneurs used joint-stock companies to finance the establishment of New World colonies.

II. THE AGE OF KINGS, 1600–1789

16. ABSOLUTISM

A system of government in which the ruler claims sole and uncontestable power. Absolute monarchs were not limited by constitutional restraints.

17. DIVINE RIGHT OF KINGS

The idea that rulers receive their authority from God and are answerable only to God. Jacques-Benigne Bossuet, a French bishop and court preacher to Louis XIV, provided the theological justification for the divine right of kings by declaring that "the state of monarchy is the supremest thing on earth, for kings are not only God's lieutenants upon earth and sit upon God's throne, but even by God himself are called gods. In the scriptures kings are called Gods, and their power is compared to the divine powers."

18. INTENDANTS

French royal officials who supervised provincial governments in the name of the king. Intendants played a key role in establishing French absolutism.

19. FRONDE

A series of rebellions against royal authority in France between 1649 and 1652. The Fronde played a key role in Louis XIV's decision to leave Paris and build the Versailles Palace.

20. ROBOT

System of forced labor used in eastern Europe. Peasants usually owed three or four days a week of forced labor. The system was abolished in 1848.

21. JUNKERS

Prussia's landowning nobility. The Junkers supported the monarchy and served in the army in exchange for absolute power over their serfs.

22. SCIENTIFIC METHOD

The use of inductive logic and controlled experiments to discover regular patterns in nature. These patterns or natural laws can be described with mathematical formulas.

23. PHILOSOPHES

Eighteenth century writers who stressed reason and advocated freedom of expression, religious toleration, and a reformed legal system. Leading philosophes such as Voltaire fought irrational prejudice and believed that society should be open to people of talent.

24. DEISM

The belief that God created the universe but allowed it to operate through the laws of nature. Deists believed that natural laws could be discovered by the use of human reason.

25. GENERAL WILL

A concept in political philosophy referring to the desire or interest of a people as a whole. As used by Jean-Jacques Rousseau, who championed the concept, the general will is identical to the rule of law.

26. ENLIGHTENED DESPOTISM

A system of government supported by leading philosophes in which an absolute ruler uses his or her power for the good of the people. Enlightened monarchs supported religious tolerance, increased economic productivity, administrative reform, and scientific academies. Joseph II, Frederick the Great, and Catherine the Great were the best-known Enlightened monarchs.

27. ENCLOSURE MOVEMENT

The process by which British landlords consolidated or fenced in common lands to increase the production of cash crops. The Enclosure Acts led to an increase in the size of farms held by large landowners.

28. AGRICULTURAL REVOLUTION

The innovations in farm production that began in eighteenth-century Holland and spread to England. These advances replaced the open-field agriculture system with a more scientific and mechanized system of agriculture.

29. PHYSIOCRATS

Group of eighteenth-century French economists led by François Quesnay. The physiocrats criticized mercantilist regulations and called for free trade.

30. INVISIBLE HAND

Phrase coined by Adam Smith to refer to the self-regulating nature of a free marketplace

III. REVOLUTION AND REACTION, 1789–1850

31. PARLEMENTS

French regional courts dominated by hereditary nobles. The Parlement of Paris claimed the right to register royal decrees before they could become law.

32. GIRONDINS

A moderate republican faction active in the French Revolution from 1791 to 1793. The Girondin Party favored a policy of extending the French Revolution beyond France's borders.

33. JACOBINS

A radical republican party during the French Revolution. Led by Maximilien Robespierre, the Jacobins unleashed the Reign of Terror. Other key leaders included Jean-Paul Marat, Georges-Jacques Danton, and the Comte de Mirabeau. The Marquis de Lafayette was not a Jacobin.

34. SANS-CULOTTES

The working people of Paris who were characterized by their long working pants and support for radical politics.

35. LEVÉE EN MASSE

The French policy of conscripting all males into the army. This created a new type of military force based upon mass participation and a fully mobilized economy.

36. THERMIDORIAN REACTION

Name given to the reaction against the radicalism of the French Revolution. It is associated with the end of the Reign of Terror and reassertion of bourgeoisie power in the Directory.

37. LEGITIMACY

The principle that rulers who have been driven from their thrones should be restored to power. For example, the Congress of Vienna restored the Bourbons to power in France.

38. BALANCE OF POWER

A strategy to maintain an equilibrium, in which weak countries join together to match or exceed the power of a stronger country. It was one of the guiding principles of the Congress of Vienna.

39. LIBERALISM

Political philosophy that in the nineteenth century advocated representative government dominated by the propertied classes, minimal government interference in the economy, religious toleration, and civil liberties such as freedom of speech.

40. CONSERVATISM

Political philosophy that in the nineteenth century supported legitimate monarchies, landed aristocracies, and established churches. Conservatives favored gradual change in the established social order.

41. NATIONALISM

Belief that a nation consists of a group of people who share similar traditions, history, and language. Nationalists argued that every nation should be sovereign and include all members of a community. A person's greatest loyalty should be to a nation-state.

42. ROMANTICISM

Philosophical and artistic movement in late eighteenth- and early nineteenth-century Europe that represented a reaction against the Neoclassical emphasis upon reason. Romantic artists, writers, and composers stressed emotion and the contemplation of nature.

43. CHARTISM

A program of political reforms sponsored by British workers in the late 1830s. Chartist demands included universal manhood suffrage, secret ballots, equal electoral districts, and salaries for members of the House of Commons.

44. ZOLLVEREIN

A free-trade union established among the major German states in 1834.

45. CARBONARI

A secret revolutionary society working to unify Italy in the 1820s.

46. LUDDITES

A social movement of British textile artisans in the early nineteenth century who protested against the changes produced by the Industrial Revolution. The Luddites believed that the new industrial machinery would eliminate their jobs. The Luddites responded by attempting to destroy the mechanized looms and other new machines.

47. UTILITARIANISM

A theory associated with Jeremy Bentham that is based upon the principle of "the greatest happiness for the greatest number." Bentham argued that this principle should be applied to each nation's government, economy, and judicial system.

48. UTOPIAN SOCIALISTS

Early nineteenth-century socialists who hoped to replace the overly competitive capitalist structure with planned communities guided by a spirit of cooperation. Leading French utopian socialists such as Charles Fourier and Louis Blanc believed that property should be communally owned.

49. MARXISM

Political and economic philosophy of Karl Marx and Friedrich Engels. They believed that history is the result of a class conflict that will end with the triumph of the industrial proletariat over the bourgeoisie. The new classless society would abolish private property.

 ## IV. TOWARD THE MODERN WORLD, 1850–1914

50. SECOND INDUSTRIAL REVOLUTION

A wave of late-nineteenth-century industrialization that was characterized by an increased use of steel, chemical processes, electric power, and railroads. This period also witnessed the spread of industrialization from Great Britain to western Europe and the United States. Both the United States and Germany soon rivaled Great Britain.

51. SOCIAL DARWINISM

The belief that there is a natural evolutionary process by which the fittest will survive. Wealthy business and industrial leaders used Social Darwinism to justify their success.

52. REALPOLITIK

"The politics of reality"; used to describe the tough, practical politics in which idealism and romanticism play no part. Otto von Bismarck and Camillo Benso di Cavour were the leading practitioners of realpolitik.

53. SYNDICALISM

A radical political movement that advocated bringing industry and government under the control of federations of labor unions. Syndicalists endorsed direct actions such as strikes and sabotage.

54. AUTOCRACY

A government in which the ruler has unlimited power and uses it in an arbitrary manner. The Romanov dynasty in Russia is the best example of an autocracy.

55. DUMA

The Russian parliament created after the revolution of 1905.

56. IMPERIALISM

The policy of extending one country's rule over other lands by conquest or economic domination.

57. SPHERE OF INFLUENCE

A region dominated by, but not directly ruled by, a foreign nation.

V. THE "SECOND THIRTY YEARS' WAR": WORLD WARS I AND II

58. FOURTEEN POINTS

President Woodrow Wilson's idealistic peace aims. Wilson stressed national self-determination, the rights of small countries, freedom of the seas, and free trade.

59. BOLSHEVIKS

A party of revolutionary Marxists, led by Vladimir Lenin, who seized power in Russia in 1917.

60. NEW ECONOMIC POLICY

A program initiated by Vladimir Lenin to stimulate the economic recovery of the Soviet Union in the early 1920s. The New Economic Policy utilized a limited revival of capitalism in light industry and agriculture.

61. EXISTENTIALISM

Philosophy that God, reason, and progress are all myths. Humans must accept responsibility for their actions. This responsibility causes an overwhelming sense of dread and anguish. Existentialism reflects the sense of isolation and alienation in the twentieth century.

62. RELATIVITY

A scientific theory associated with Albert Einstein. Relativity holds that time and space do not exist separately. Instead, they are a combined continuum whose measurement depends as much on the observer as on the entities being measured.

63. TOTALITARIANISM

A political system in which the government has total control over the lives of individual citizens.

64. FASCISM

A political system that combines an authoritarian government with a corporate economy. Fascist governments glorify their leaders, appeal to nationalism, control the media, and repress individual liberties.

65. KULAKS

Prosperous landowning peasants in czarist Russia. Joseph Stalin accused the kulaks of being class enemies of the poorer peasants. Stalin "liquidated the kulaks as a class" by executing them and expropriating their land to form collective farms.

66. KEYNESIAN ECONOMICS

An economic theory based on the ideas of twentieth-century British economist John Maynard Keynes. According to Keynesian economics, governments can spend their economies out of a depression by using deficit-spending to encourage employment and stimulate economic growth.

67. APPEASEMENT

A policy of making concessions to an aggressor in the hopes of avoiding war. Associated with Neville Chamberlain's policy of making concessions to Adolf Hitler.

VI. THE COLD WAR ERA, 1945–1991

68. CONTAINMENT

The name of a U.S. foreign policy designed to contain or block the spread of Soviet policy. Inspired by George F. Kennan, containment was expressed in the Truman Doctrine and implemented in the Marshall Plan and the North American Treaty Organization (NATO) alliance.

69. DECOLONIZATION

The process by which colonies gained their independence from the imperial European powers after World War II.

70. DE-STALINIZATION

The policy of liberalization of the Stalinist system in the Soviet Union. As carried out by Nikita Khrushchev, de-Stalinization meant denouncing Joseph Stalin's cult of personality, producing more consumer goods, allowing greater cultural freedom, and pursuing peaceful coexistence with the West.

71. BREZHNEV DOCTRINE

Assertion that the Soviet Union and its allies had the right to intervene in any socialist country whenever they saw the need. The

Brezhnev Doctrine justified the Soviet invasion of Czechoslovakia in 1968.

72. DÉTENTE

The relaxation of tensions between the United States and the Soviet Union. Détente was introduced by Secretary of State Henry Kissinger and President Richard Nixon. Examples of détente include the Strategic Arms Limitation Talks (SALT), expanded trade with the Soviet Union, and President Nixon's trips to China and Russia.

73. SOLIDARITY

A Polish labor union founded in 1980 by Lech Walesa and Anna Walentynowicz. Solidarity contested Communist Party programs and eventually ousted the party from the Polish government.

74. GLASNOST

Policy initiated by Soviet premier Mikhail Gorbachev in the mid-1980s. Glasnost resulted in a new openness of speech, reduced censorship, and greater criticism of Communist Party policies.

75. PERESTROIKA

An economic policy initiated by Soviet premier Mikhail Gorbachev in the mid-1980s. Meaning "restructuring," perestroika called for less government regulation and greater efficiency in manufacturing and agriculture.

76. WELFARE STATE

A social system in which the state assumes primary responsibility for the welfare of its citizens in matters of health care, education, employment, and social security. Germany was the first European country to develop a state social welfare system.

PART II:

CHRONOLOGICAL Review

The Italian Renaissance

I. RISE OF THE ITALIAN CITY-STATES

A. URBAN CENTERS

1. While the rest of Europe was still rural, a number of cities prospered in northern Italy.
2. By the late 1300s, Florence, Venice, and Milan all had populations of about 100,000.

B. WEALTHY MERCHANTS

1. In the absence of hereditary kings, wealthy merchants formed oligarchies that governed the independent city-states in northern Italy.
2. Wealthy merchant families dominated political, economic, and artistic life in the northern Italian cities.

II. FLORENCE AND THE MEDICI

A. THE PRIMACY OF FLORENCE

1. During the fifteenth century or *Quattrocento*, Florence became the acknowledged center of the Renaissance—the rebirth of classical learning, literature, and art.
2. The golden age of Florence was based on the wealth earned by its textile merchants and bankers.

B. THE LEADERSHIP OF THE MEDICI

1. The Medici family dominated Florence's economic, political, and artistic life for much of the fifteenth century.

2. The Medici earned their wealth as bankers. Led by Cosimo (1389–1464), Piero (1416–1469), and Lorenzo the Magnificent (1449–1492), the Medici financed libraries, built churches, sponsored the Platonic Academy of Philosophy, and commissioned hundreds of artworks.

3. The Florentine Renaissance reached its peak during the lifetime of Lorenzo the Magnificent.

III. THE RENAISSANCE SPIRIT

A. THE MEDIEVAL MIND-SET

1. Medieval thinkers believed that God had created the world to prepare humans for salvation or eternal damnation. Human beings and their lives on earth were equally insignificant. The individual was of no importance.

2. Medieval artists did not win fame as individuals. The architects, glassmakers, and sculptors who designed and decorated Europe's great cathedrals worked for the glory of God, not for personal glory.

B. A NEW CELEBRATION OF THE INDIVIDUAL

1. Unlike feudal nobles, Italian merchants did not inherit their social rank. Success in business depended mostly on the merchants' own skill. As a result, prosperous merchants took pride in their achievements. They believed they were successful because of their merit as individuals.

2. Like the merchants, northern Italian artists and writers were eager to be known and remembered as individuals. From this time on, we know the names of people who created works of art. Fame thus became a reward for superior talent.

3. Portrait painting and autobiography illustrate the interest in individual personality and fame. Wealthy patrons wanted their portraits recorded for posterity. Renaissance artists often included self-portraits in their paintings. Autobiographies were the written equivalents of self-portraits.

4. Renaissance individualism stressed the importance of personality, the development of unique talents, and the pursuit of fame and glory. By displaying the full range of human abilities, a Renaissance person demonstrated the highly-prized trait known as *virtu*.

5. In his famous *Oration on the Dignity of Man*, Giovanni Pico della Mirandola celebrated the human potential for greatness.

C. SCHOLARSHIP AND THE LOVE OF CLASSICAL LEARNING

1. Petrarch and other Renaissance scholars scorned medieval art and literature. Petrarch summed up the Renaissance attitude by calling the medieval years "the Dark Ages."

2. Scholars such as Petrarch who studied the classical texts and cultures of ancient Greece and Rome were called humanists.

3. Inspired by classical authors, humanists rejected medieval scholasticism and instead advocated a curriculum based on the study of Greek and Roman literature, rhetoric, and history. Humanists believed that by studying the classics they would gain a more practical understanding of human nature.

4. Humanists played a key role in promoting the new liberal arts education, developing vernacular languages, and renewing interest in translating and preserving Greek and Roman manuscripts.

5. Lorenzo Valla demonstrated the power of Renaissance scholarship when he used a careful linguistic and historical analysis to demonstrate that the Donation of Constantine was actually a clumsy forgery.

D. A NEW SECULAR SPIRIT

1. Medieval culture emphasized spiritual values and salvation.

2. Renaissance culture was far more interested in the pleasures of material possessions. Wealthy Renaissance families openly enjoyed fine music, expensive foods, and beautiful works of art.

IV. EDUCATION AND THE IDEAL COURTIER

A. HUMANIST EDUCATION

1. Medieval scholastics studied the classics to understand God. In contrast, Renaissance humanists studied the classics to understand human nature and learn practical skills.
2. Leading humanists opened schools and academies that taught Roman history, Greek philosophy, and Latin grammar and rhetoric.
3. Humanists believed that their classical curriculum would teach future business, political, and military leaders how to become eloquent and persuasive speakers and writers.

B. BALDASSARE CASTIGLIONE (1478–1529)

1. For Renaissance humanists, the ideal individual strove to become a "universal man" who excelled in many fields.
2. In his book *The Courtier*, Baldassare Castiglione explained how upper-class men and women could become accomplished courtiers.
3. According to Castiglione, the ideal courtier should be polite, charming, and witty. He should be able to dance, write poetry, sing, and play music. In addition, he should be physically graceful and strong.
4. Castiglione did not ignore upper-class women. The perfect court lady, he said, should be well educated and charming. Yet women were not expected to seek fame as men did. Like Dante's Beatrice and Petrarch's Laura, they were expected to inspire poetry and art but rarely to create it.

 V. MACHIAVELLI AND *THE PRINCE*

A. TURMOIL IN ITALY

1. The golden age of Florence lasted nearly a century. Lorenzo the Magnificent's unexpected death in 1492 left Florence without a strong leader.

2. In 1494, King Charles VIII of France invaded Italy with the goal of conquering Naples. Spain's King Ferdinand soon contested the French claim to Naples.

3. These invasions sparked a series of conflicts called the Habsburg-Valois Wars that involved all the major Italian city-states. Diplomacy and war became the keys to survival.

B. NICCOLÒ MACHIAVELLI (1469–1527)

1. Machiavelli was a Florentine diplomat and political philosopher. He is considered the founder of modern political science.

2. Machiavelli was appalled by the devastation caused by the Habsburg-Valois Wars. "At this time," he passionately wrote, "the whole land of Italy is without a head, without order, beaten, spoiled, torn in pieces, overrun, and abandoned to destruction in every shape. She prays God to send someone to rescue her from these barbarous cruelties."

3. Machiavelli wrote *The Prince* to advise Italian rulers on the ruthless statecraft needed to unite his war-torn and divided Italian homeland.

C. THE QUALITIES OF A SUCCESSFUL PRINCE

1. Machiavelli had a pessimistic view of human nature. He believed that people are "ungrateful, changeable, simulators and dissimulators, runaways in danger, eager for gain; while you do well by them they are all yours; they offer you their blood, their property, their lives, their children when need is far off; but when it comes near you, they turn about."

2. Because human nature is selfish, untrustworthy, and corrupt, a prince must be strong as a lion and shrewd as a fox: "For the lion cannot protect himself from traps, and the fox cannot defend himself from wolves. One must therefore be a fox to recognize traps, and a lion to fight wolves."

3. The successful ruler, Machiavelli insisted, must be ruthless and pragmatic, always remembering that the end justifies the means.

CHRONOLOGICAL REVIEW

VI. ITALIAN RENAISSANCE ART

A. PATRONS

1. Renaissance artists were not independent contractors who produced works of art for themselves or the public. Instead, they received commissions from the Catholic Church, guilds, and wealthy families such as the Medici.
2. While these patrons appreciated the beauty of fine art, they also understood the ability of artists to create visible symbols of power. Renaissance patrons thus used art as a way of displaying their wealth and promoting their fame.

B. CHARACTERISTICS OF RENAISSANCE ART

1. Perspective
    ▸ *Perspective is a geometric method of creating the illusion of depth on a flat, two-dimensional surface.*
    ▸ *Perspective enabled artists to create paintings that opened "a window on the world." This way of presenting space became the foundation of European painting for the next 500 years.*
2. Chiaroscuro
    ▸ *Chiaroscuro is the realistic blending of light and shade to model forms.*
    ▸ *Chiaroscuro creates the illusion of volume.*
    ▸ *Chiaroscuro and perspective enabled artists to create paintings in which real people seemed to occupy real space.*

3. Pyramid configuration
   ▸ *Byzantine and medieval art featured flat, rigid figures arranged in a horizontal line.*
   ▸ *Renaissance artists used three-dimensional pyramid configurations to create symmetrical and balanced compositions.*
4. Classical forms and Christian subjects
   ▸ *Inspired by their study of Greek and Roman statues, Renaissance artists attempted to revive classical standards of beauty.*
   ▸ *It is important to remember that Renaissance artists did not abandon Christian themes and subjects. Rather, Renaissance art often combined classical forms with Christian subjects.*

You do not need to memorize a long list of Renaissance artists and their works of art. Instead, focus on key masterpieces that illustrate Renaissance ideals and the impact of humanism. The three works described in this section are designed to provide you with a handy list of examples for free-response essay questions on the Italian Renaissance.

C. KEY EXAMPLES OF RENAISSANCE ART AND ARCHITECTURE

1. Leon Battista Alberti, *The West Façade of Sant' Andrea*
   ▸ *Alberti broke with medieval traditions by eliminating statues and other traditional features of Gothic architecture.*
   ▸ *Alberti's ambitious design featured a Roman triumphal arch framed by colossal Corinthian pilasters. The pilasters supported a pediment inspired by classical temples.*
   ▸ *Sant' Andrea marked a decisive break with Christian building traditions. By achieving the Renaissance ideal of combining ancient forms with Christian uses, Alberti created a "Christian temple" that strongly influenced the design of future Renaissance and baroque churches.*

2. Michelangelo, *David*

  ▸ *David's* contrapposto *(stiff right leg and relaxed left leg) pose recalls statues from Greece and Rome.*
  ▸ *Like many classical statues,* David *is a nude. However, unlike the serene classical statues,* David *defiantly faces Goliath. His muscular body is tense with gathering power as God's champion prepares for battle.*

3. Raphael, *The School of Athens*

  ▸ *The* School of Athens *depicts a gathering of ancient philosophers from various eras. The sages seem to move freely in a carefully designed three-dimensional space.*
  ▸ *The toga-clad figures of Plato and Aristotle dominate the center of the painting.*
  ▸ *Raphael underscored the rising status of Renaissance artists by including portraits of his contemporaries among the ancient philosophers. For example, Plato is a portrait of Leonardo da Vinci. Raphael also included a portrait of himself on the far right, looking out at the viewer.*
  ▸ *The* School of Athens *brilliantly illustrates the Renaissance ideals of order, unity, and symmetry.*

VII. WOMEN DURING THE RENAISSANCE

A. THE DEBATE ABOUT WOMEN

1. The beginning of the Renaissance coincided with a "debate about women" (*querelle des femmes*).
2. Humanist scholars and others debated women's character, nature, and role in society.

B. CHRISTINE DE PIZAN (1364–1430), THE FIRST FEMINIST

1. Pizan was a prolific writer who became the first woman in European history to earn a living as an author.
2. Pizan wrote a history of famous women designed to refute "masculine myths" about women. She is now remembered as Europe's first feminist.

C. CASTIGLIONE AND THE PERFECT COURT LADY

1. As mentioned earlier, Castiglione believed the perfect court lady should be attractive, well educated, and able to paint, dance, and play a musical instrument.
2. Although well educated, Castiglione's court lady was not expected to actively participate in political, artistic, or literary affairs. Instead, she should be a pleasing and attractive "ornament" for her upper-class husband.

D. ISABELLA D'ESTE (1475–1539), THE FIRST LADY OF THE RENAISSANCE

1. Isabella d'Este was the most famous Renaissance woman.
2. She was born into the ruling family of Ferrara and married the ruler of Mantua.
3. She was an art patron whose collection included works by many of the greatest Renaissance artists.
4. Her life illustrates that becoming a patron of the arts was the most socially acceptable role for a well-educated Renaissance woman.

The Northern Renaissance

 I. **THE NORTHERN RENAISSANCE**

A. CONTACT WITH THE ITALIAN RENAISSANCE

1. During the late 1400s, students and artists from northern Europe traveled to Italy where they became acquainted with the "new learning" and the new style of painting.
2. At the same time, merchants from the Low Countries, France, Germany, and England also visited Italy and learned about the advances of the Italian Renaissance.

B. CHRISTIAN HUMANISM

1. Northern humanists were often called Christian humanists. Like their Italian counterparts, the Christian humanists closely studied classical sources. However, they also sought to give humanism a specifically Christian content.
2. Christian humanists wanted to combine the classical ideals of calmness and stoical patience with the Christian virtues of piety, humility, and love. They believed that this fusion would create the best code of virtuous conduct.
3. Christian humanists were committed to moral and institutional reform.

It is important to understand the difference between Italian humanists and Northern humanists. While both studied classical texts, the Northern humanists also studied early Christian texts and were far more concerned with religious piety than their Italian counterparts.

KEY FIGURES IN THE NORTHERN RENAISSANCE

A. DESIDERIUS ERASMUS (1466–1536)

1. Known as the "prince of the humanists," Erasmus was the most famous and influential humanist of the Northern Renaissance.

2. The greatest scholar of his age, Erasmus edited the works of the church fathers and produced Greek and Latin editions of the New Testament.

3. Erasmus is best known for writing *The Praise of Folly*, a witty satire that poked fun at greedy merchants, pompous priests, and quarrelsome scholars. Erasmus saved his most stinging barbs for the immorality and hypocrisy of church leaders, including Pope Julius II.

4. Erasmus was a devout Catholic committed to reforming the church from within. It is important to note the Erasmus saw himself as a teacher of morality who wanted to reform the church, not destroy it.

5. While most humanists wrote in the vernacular, Erasmus continued to write in Latin.

B. THOMAS MORE (1478–1535)

1. More was the leading humanist scholar in England. A renowned author, lawyer, and statesman, More held many high public offices including lord chancellor under Henry VIII.

2. More is best known for writing *Utopia* (meaning "Nowhere"), a novel describing an imaginary society located somewhere off the mainland of the New World. The country of Utopia featured religious toleration, a humanist education for both men and women, and communal ownership of property.

C. MICHEL DE MONTAIGNE (1533–1592)

1. Montaigne was one of the most influential writers of the French Renaissance.

2. He is best known for popularizing the essay as a literary genre. Montaigne's writings feature numerous vivid

anecdotes and a skeptical tone best illustrated by his famous question, *Que sais-je?* ("What do I know?").

III. THE PRINTING REVOLUTION

A. JOHANNES GUTENBERG AND THE PRINTING PRESS

1. Johannes Gutenberg is credited with inventing the first printing press with movable type. In 1456, the first full work ever printed by movable type, the Mazarin Bible, was published.
2. Printing quickly spread across Europe. By 1500, presses in over 200 cities printed between 8 million and 20 million books, far more than the number of books produced in all of previous Western history.

B. IMPACT OF THE PRINTING PRESS

1. The printing press enabled the works of humanists such as Erasmus and More to be quickly disseminated across Europe.
2. The profusion of printing technology made it difficult for authorities to suppress dissenting views.

The printing press had a revolutionary impact upon European life and thought. APEURO test writers often compose essay questions asking students to describe and analyze how the printing press altered European culture between 1450 and 1600. It is important to note that like today's Internet, the printing press promoted freedom of expression, disseminated information, and challenged the power of established authorities to control divergent views.

IV. NORTHERN RENAISSANCE ART

A. CHARACTERISTICS

1. Northern Renaissance artists were the first to use and perfect oil painting.

2. The new oil paints enabled Renaissance artists to paint reality precisely as it appeared. Their works are renowned for meticulous details of everyday objects.

3. Many of the everyday objects in Northern Renaissance paintings are actually disguised symbols. For example, in *The Arnolfini Wedding*, the dog represents fidelity and the discarded shoes are a sign that a religious ceremony is taking place. It is interesting to note that people believed that touching the ground with bare feet ensured fertility.

B. KEY ARTISTS

1. Jan van Eyck (1390–1441)
   ▶ *Van Eyck was the most acclaimed Flemish artist of the fifteenth century.*
   ▶ *He was one of the pioneers in oil painting.*
   ▶ *Van Eyck is best known for the* Ghent Altarpiece *and* The Arnolfini Wedding.

2. Albrecht Dürer (1471–1528)
   ▶ *Dürer was the first Northern Renaissance artist to fully absorb the innovations of the Italian Renaissance.*
   ▶ *He is best known for his woodcuts and self-portraits.*

3. Hans Holbein the Younger (1497–1543)
   ▶ *Like Dürer, Holbein blended the Northern Renaissance's love of precise realism with the Italian Renaissance's love of balanced proportion and perspective.*
   ▶ *His best-known works are his realistic portraits of Henry VIII and Thomas More.*

V. THE NEW MONARCHS

A. CHARACTERISTICS OF MEDIEVAL KINGS

1. Medieval kings received most of their income from their own estates and from grants of money from their vassals.

2. Medieval kings marched to war followed by an army of vassals who owed military service in exchange for land.

3. Medieval kings relied upon nobles for advice and counsel.

4. Medieval kings shared power with the church and were often subordinate to the pope.

B. CHARACTERISTICS OF THE NEW MONARCHS

1. The new monarchs retained their feudal income while also taxing towns, merchants, and peasants.

2. The new monarchs created professional armies that were paid from the royal treasury.

3. The new monarchs created a more centralized administrative bureaucracy that relied upon educated and loyal middle-class officials.

4. The new monarchs negotiated a new relationship with the Catholic Church.

C. FRANCE

1. Charles VII (reigned 1422–1461)

   ▸ *Charles VII successfully concluded the Hundred Years' War by expelling the English from France.*

   ▸ *He strengthened royal finances through such taxes as the taille (on land) and the gabelle (on salt). These two taxes were the main source of royal income for the next three centuries.*

   ▸ *He created the first permanent royal army.*

2. Louis XI (reigned 1461–1483)

   ▸ *Louis XI further enlarged the royal army.*

   ▸ *He encouraged economic growth by promoting new industries such as silk weaving.*

3. Francis I (reigned 1515–1547)

   ▸ *Francis I was the first French king to be called "Your Majesty."*

   ▸ *He reached an agreement with Pope Leo X known as the Concordat of Bologna (1516), which authorized the king to nominate bishops, abbots, and other high officials of the Catholic Church in France. This agreement gave the French monarch administrative control over the church.*

D. ENGLAND

1. Henry VII (reigned 1485–1509)
   ▸ *Henry VII created a special court known as the Star Chamber as a political weapon to try prominent nobles. Court sessions were held in secret with no right of appeal, no juries, and no witnesses.*
   ▸ *He used justices of the peace to extend royal authority into the local shires.*
   ▸ *He encouraged the wool industry and expanded the English merchant marine.*
2. Henry VIII (reigned 1509–1547)
   ▸ *Henry VIII declared the king the supreme head of the Church of England, thus severing England's ties with the Catholic Church.*
   ▸ *He dissolved the monasteries and confiscated their land and wealth.*

E. SPAIN

1. The Iberian Peninsula in the mid-fifteenth century
   ▸ *During this time, the Iberian Peninsula enjoyed a rich cultural diversity that included prominent Jewish and Muslim communities.*
   ▸ *The kingdoms of Castile and Aragon dominated Navarre and Portugal. The Muslims held only the small kingdom of Granada.*
2. Ferdinand (reigned 1479–1516) and Isabella (reigned 1474–1504)
   ▸ *The marriage of Ferdinand of Aragon and Isabella of Castile (1469) created a dynastic union of the Iberian Peninsula's two most powerful royal houses.*
   ▸ *Ferdinand and Isabella reduced the number of nobles on the royal council.*
   ▸ *Ferdinand and Isabella completed the Reconquista by conquering Granada and incorporating it into the Spanish kingdom.*

▸ *Isabella decreed that in a Christian state, there could be only "one king, one law, one faith." She and Ferdinand established the Inquisition to enforce religious conformity.*

▸ *In 1492, Ferdinand and Isabella issued an edict expelling all practicing Jews from Spain. Ten years later, they demanded that all Muslims adopt Christianity or leave Spain.*

F. CONSEQUENCES

1. The new monarchs consolidated royal power and created the foundation for modern nation-states in France, England, and Spain.
2. It is important to remember that the new monarchs did not gain absolute power. The age of absolutism would not occur until the seventeenth century.

The Reformation

I. LUTHERANISM

A. MARTIN LUTHER'S PERSONAL QUEST FOR SALVATION

1. Luther's early life was dominated by a private struggle to find the key to personal salvation.

2. The Catholic Church taught that salvation could be achieved by both good works and faith. For many long years, Luther struggled to follow this dual path to salvation. However, he was overwhelmed by a deep sense of personal guilt.

3. After many years of study, Luther began to examine St. Paul's Letter to the Romans. One evening, Luther read Paul's admonition that "the just shall be saved by faith."

4. Luther's arduous years of study prepared him for this fateful moment. At last he understood that salvation was a gift freely given by God.

B. NINETY-FIVE THESES

1. Luther's spiritual journey seemed to culminate in a personal revelation. But then historic events intersected with his life.

2. In 1517, Luther witnessed Johann Tetzel selling indulgences near Wittenberg. In Luther's time, an indulgence was a certificate granted by the pope in return for the payment of a fee to the church. The certificate stated that the soul of the dead relative or friend of the purchaser would have his time in purgatory reduced by many years or cancelled altogether.

3. Part of the income from the indulgences sold by Tetzel was destined for Rome to help pay for the construction of the new St. Peter's Basilica.

4. Tetzel's aggressive marketing tactics appalled Luther. He believed that salvation could not be sold by the pope; it was a free gift given by God.

5. On October 31, 1517, Luther dramatically nailed his Ninety-five Theses to the door of Castle Church in Wittenberg. Aided by the printing press, Luther's defiant challenge was soon disseminated across Europe. Within a short time, he became the most famous and controversial person in Europe.

C. LUTHER'S KEY BELIEFS

1. Salvation is achieved by faith alone.
   - *The Catholic Church had long taught that salvation could be achieved by both faith and good works.*
   - *Luther insisted that faith was the only path to salvation.*

2. The Bible is the only valid authority for Christian life.
   - *The Catholic Church taught that authority rests in both the Bible and the traditional teachings of the church.*
   - *Luther insisted that all church teachings should be based on the Word of God as revealed in the Bible.*
   - *Based upon his study of the Bible, Luther argued that Christ established just two sacraments: baptism and the Eucharist or holy communion. Luther thus rejected the Catholic teaching that there were seven sacraments.*

3. The church consists of a priesthood of all believers.
   - *The Roman Catholic Church was a hierarchical organization led by the pope.*
   - *Luther insisted that because all Christians are spiritually equal, the church consists of the entire community of the Christian faithful.*

4. All vocations have equal merit.
   - *The Catholic Church taught that the monastic life was superior to the secular life.*
   - *Luther rejected this belief, arguing that all honest work has equal merit. Each person should serve God in his or her own individual calling.*
   - *Luther abolished monasteries and convents. He declared that the clergy should marry.*

D. THE GERMAN PEASANTS' WAR, 1525

1. Causes
   - ▶ *German peasants originally supported Luther. They heard his message as one that promised freedom from oppression by the landlords and the clergy.*
   - ▶ *Complaints that nobles had seized village common lands and imposed exorbitant rents soon escalated to open attacks on monasteries, castles, and prosperous farms.*

2. Luther's response
   - ▶ *The peasants believed Luther would support them. Luther, however, believed that Christians ought to obey their rulers—even unjust rulers—and that rebellion against the state was always wrong and must be crushed.*
   - ▶ *Horrified at the prospect of a bloody revolution, Luther urged the German nobility to crush the rebels.*

3. Consequences
   - ▶ *The German Peasants' War of 1525 strengthened the authority of the German nobility.*
   - ▶ *Lutheranism became closely allied with the established political order controlled by the German nobility.*

Test Tip

It is easy to focus on Luther's dramatic stand against indulgences while ignoring his response to the German Peasants' War. Don't make this mistake. The German Peasants' War has been featured on several multiple-choice questions and was the topic of the 2008 DBQ (see Chapter 27). In addition, it can be used in free-response essay questions discussing the political and social consequences of the Protestant Reformation.

E. LUTHER AND THE ROLE OF CHRISTIAN WOMEN

1. The elimination of monasteries and convents was a key factor in changing the role of sixteenth-century women.
2. Luther believed that Christian women should strive to be models of obedience and Christian charity.

F. THE SPREAD OF LUTHERANISM

1. Lutheranism became the dominant religion in northern and eastern Germany. It is important to remember that most of southern Germany, Austria, and the Rhineland remained Roman Catholic.

2. Lutheranism became the predominant religion in Denmark and Scandinavia.

G. THE PEACE OF AUGSBURG, 1555

1. Between 1546 and 1555, a religious civil war between Catholics led by Charles V and Protestants led by German princes tore Germany apart. It is important to note that the Catholic king of France supported the Protestant nobles. This is an example of the long-standing French policy of maintaining a divided Germany.

2. The Peace of Augsburg ended the civil war. The settlement gave each German prince the right to determine the religion of his state, either Roman Catholic or Lutheran. The Peace of Augsburg did not provide for the recognition of Calvinists and other religious minorities.

H. WAS LUTHER A REVOLUTIONARY OR A CONSERVATIVE?

1. Luther was a religious revolutionary.
    ▸ *Luther's core beliefs went well beyond attempting to reform the Roman Catholic Church. His doctrines of justification by faith, priesthood of all believers, and the Bible as the sole authority marked a major departure from long-standing Catholic principles.*
    ▸ *Luther's revolutionary actions included abolishing monasteries, reducing the number of sacraments, encouraging priests to marry, and repudiating the pope's authority to interpret the Bible.*

2. Luther was a political conservative.
    ▸ *Luther insisted that Christians owed obedience to established authority.*
    ▸ *Luther gave his support to the German nobility as they brutally suppressed the peasant rebellion.*

CALVINISM

A. JOHN CALVIN'S KEY BELIEFS

1. Calvin's doctrines are clearly and systematically explained in his landmark book, *The Institutes of the Christian Religion*.
2. Calvin asserted that while God is just, perfect, and omnipotent, humans are corrupt, weak, and insignificant.
3. Since men and women are by nature sinful, they cannot actively work to achieve salvation. Because God is all-knowing, he has "determined, both whom he would admit to salvation and whom he would condemn to destruction." This "terrible decree" constitutes the theological principle called predestination.
4. By God's grace, a very few people will be saved from sin. Calvin called these people the "elect."
5. Calvin taught that the elect have a duty to rule society so as to glorify God. The ideal government should therefore be a theocracy in which church leaders dominate civil authorities.
6. Calvin and Luther agreed on many fundamental points of theology. However, they disagreed on the emphasis placed upon predestination and the relationship between church and civil authorities. While Luther believed that the church should be subordinated to the state, Calvin stressed that the elect have a duty to Christianize the state.

B. GENEVA, "CITY OF SAINTS"

1. In 1541, Protestants in Geneva, Switzerland, asked Calvin to transform their city into a model Christian community.
2. Calvin and his followers regulated all aspects of life in Geneva. They suppressed frivolous activities such as playing cards, dancing, and attending the theater. At the same time, they strictly enforced a high standard of morality that included regular church attendance.

C. THE SPREAD OF CALVINISM

1. Protestant reformers from France, England, and Scotland hailed Calvin's Geneva as "the most perfect school of Christ

CHRONOLOGICAL REVIEW

since the days of the Apostles." Geneva thus became both the center of Calvin's reformed church and a compelling model for other Protestant leaders.

2. In the late 1550s, John Knox brought Calvinism to Scotland. Within a decade, the Presbyterian Church founded by Knox and his followers became the basis for Scotland's established religion.

3. Calvinism soon spread to France, where followers were called Huguenots.

4. Calvinists also founded Puritan churches in England and later in New England.

III. ANGLICANISM

A. HENRY VIII (REIGNED 1509–1547)

1. The "Defender of the Faith"
    ▸ *Henry VIII was a devout Catholic who detested Luther.*
    ▸ *Henry wrote a pamphlet calling Luther "a great limb of the Devil." Impressed by Henry's loyalty, the pope gave him a special title, "Defender of the Faith."*

2. The problem of succession
    ▸ *Henry's political needs proved more important than his loyalty to the pope.*
    ▸ *Since Henry was only the second king of the Tudor dynasty, he was determined to have a male heir. When his wife, Catherine of Aragon, failed to give birth to a son, Henry asked Pope Clement VII to annul the marriage.*
    ▸ *The pope would normally have granted Henry's request. However, Catherine of Aragon was the aunt of the Holy Roman Emperor Charles V. At the time of Henry's request, Charles's armies controlled Rome. Caught between the plea of a distant English king and the immediate presence of a powerful Holy Roman emperor, the pope delayed and finally refused to annul Henry's marriage.*

3. The Act of Supremacy, 1534
    ▸ *Thwarted by the pope, Henry turned to a radical solution to solve his marriage problem.*

▸ *In 1533, Henry defied the pope and married Anne Boleyn.*

▸ *The following year, Parliament passed the Act of Supremacy. This landmark act declared the English king to be the "Protector and Only Supreme Head of the Church and Clergy of England."*

▸ *Although Henry VIII rejected papal supremacy, he remained a devout Catholic. In 1539, Parliament approved the Six Articles defining the doctrine of the English Church. With the sole exception of papal supremacy, the Six Articles reaffirmed Catholic teachings while rejecting Protestant beliefs.*

4. Dissolution of the monasteries

▸ *Beginning in 1536, Parliament passed acts closing all English monasteries and seizing their lands.*

▸ *Henry sold much of the land to nobles and to members of England's increasingly prosperous merchant class.*

▸ *Enriched by the monastic lands, these groups became loyal supporters of the Tudor dynasty.*

B. MAKING COMPARISONS: HENRY VIII AND MARTIN LUTHER

1. On first glance, Henry VIII and Martin Luther had very little in common. Henry rejected Luther's core doctrines, and the two exchanged derisive pamphlets filled with insults. Guided by his faith, Luther wanted to reform and then change the Catholic Church. Guided by his dynastic interests, Henry wanted a male heir in order to avoid a potentially bloody succession.

2. Henry VIII and Martin Luther had very different religious beliefs and motives. Nonetheless, they shared similar political attitudes. Both believed that the church should be subordinate to the state. Both Henry VIII and Martin Luther rejected papal authority. In addition, both followed policies intended to strengthen the nobility. As we have seen, Luther supported the nobility by encouraging them to suppress the rebellious peasants. Henry supported the nobility by allowing them to purchase monastic lands.

C. ELIZABETH I (REIGNED 1558–1603)

1. Religious issues
   - *Elizabeth I inherited a difficult religious problem. Since Henry VIII's break with Rome in 1534, royal religious policy had changed direction several times.*
   - *Protestants gained strength under Edward VI (reigned 1547–1553). Catholics experienced a renewal under Mary (reigned 1553–1558).*

2. The Elizabethan Settlement
   - *Elizabeth was a politique who placed political necessities above her personal beliefs. She therefore strove to find a middle course that moderate Catholics and moderate Protestants would accept.*
   - *The Elizabethan Settlement restored the Church of England. Also known as the Anglican Church, the Church of England allowed priests to marry and to conduct sermons in English. However, the Church of England retained archbishops and bishops who wore elaborate robes and conducted services that remained formal and traditional.*
   - *Although Protestant in tone, the Church of England instituted dogmas that were deliberately broad and often ambiguous.*

D. <u>MAKING COMPARISONS</u>: ISABELLA OF SPAIN AND ELIZABETH I OF ENGLAND

1. Both Queen Isabella of Spain and Queen Elizabeth I of England shared the goal of ruling over a united country. However, they followed dramatically different religious policies to achieve this goal.

2. Isabella was a devout Roman Catholic who decreed that in a Christian state, there could be only "one king, one law, one faith." She revived the Inquisition, conquered Muslim-controlled Grenada, and forced Jews and Muslims to become Christians or leave Spain. Her actions created religious unity but at the price of harming Spain's economy.

3. Elizabeth was a politique. Although raised a Protestant, her religious views are largely unknown. What mattered most to

Elizabeth was not the religious beliefs of her subjects but their loyalty. She wanted to avoid destructive religious civil wars. It was not her intention, she said, "to pry windows into men's souls." Elizabeth's reign marked the beginning of a cultural golden age and a period of sustained economic growth and prosperity.

IV. ANABAPTISM

A. ANABAPTIST BELIEFS

1. Anabaptists, or rebaptizers, opposed infant baptism, insisting that only adult baptism conformed to Scripture.
2. Anabaptists advocated complete separation of church and state.

B. ANABAPTIST LEADERS

1. Catholics, Lutherans, and Calvinists all condemned Anabaptist leaders as radicals.
2. Modern historians have labeled Thomas Munzer a "left wing" Anabaptist leader because he advocated the overthrow of the existing political and social order. Munzer was executed in 1525.

Most texts focus on comparing and contrasting the religious views of Luther and Calvin while devoting little attention to the Anabaptists. Don't neglect the Anabaptists. APEURO test writers expect you to know that the Anabaptists advocated the complete separation of church and state.

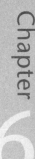

The Catholic Reformation and the Wars of Religion

Chapter 6

CHRONOLOGICAL REVIEW

 I. THE CATHOLIC REFORMATION

A. THE REFORMATION POPES

1. Renaissance popes such as Julius II concentrated their energies on commissioning art, building a new St. Peter's, and enhancing the power of their own families.
2. Beginning with Pope Paul III (1534–1549), a new generation of popes committed themselves to appointing reform-minded officials, enforcing strict moral standards, and creating new religious orders.

B. THE COUNCIL OF TRENT

1. Reaffirmed Catholic doctrines
   - *The Council of Trent rejected Luther's doctrine of justification by faith and reaffirmed that salvation is achieved by both faith and good works.*
   - *The council rejected the Protestant belief in the supremacy of the Bible and reaffirmed that equal weight should be given to Scripture and to traditional Catholic teachings.*
   - *It rejected Luther's contention that there were just two sacraments and reaffirmed that there were seven sacraments.*
2. Reformed church abuses
   - *The council decreed that indulgences should no longer be sold in exchange for financial contributions.*
   - *It forbade simony, the sale of church offices.*
   - *The council instructed bishops to live in the dioceses they served.*

3. Reasserted traditional practices
   ▸ *The council reaffirmed the veneration of relics and images as valid expressions of Christian piety.*
   ▸ *It confirmed the Vulgate as the authoritative Catholic edition of the Bible.*
   ▸ *It decreed that Latin continue to be the language of worship.*

4. Resisted limiting papal authority
   ▸ *The council ruled that no act of a council could be valid unless accepted by the Holy See.*
   ▸ *It preserved the papacy as the center of Catholic unity.*

C. THE JESUITS

1. Ignatius Loyola (1491–1556)
   ▸ *Ignatius was an unknown Spanish soldier who suffered a severe injury while fighting the French.*
   ▸ *During his recovery, Ignatius experienced a religious conversion. He resolved to become a soldier of Christ and dedicate his life to fighting for the pope and the Catholic Church.*

2. Society of Jesus
   ▸ *In 1540, Pope Paul III formally authorized the Society of Jesus. Those who joined were called Jesuits.*
   ▸ *Led by Ignatius, the Jesuits were a spiritual army that emphasized iron discipline and absolute obedience.*
   ▸ *Ignatius wrote* The Spiritual Exercises, *detailing a system of disciplined meditation, prayer, and study.*

3. Activities of the Jesuits
   ▸ *Catholic education: Jesuits founded hundreds of schools for middle- and upper-class boys. Jesuits were especially prominent as confessors and advisors to royal families.*
   ▸ *Missionary work: Jesuit missionaries played a key role in preaching Christianity in the Americas and Asia.*
   ▸ *Combating Protestantism: Jesuits spearheaded the revival of Catholicism in Bavaria, the southern Netherlands, and Poland.*

II. BAROQUE ART

A. PURPOSE OF BAROQUE ART

1. The Protestant Reformation represented the greatest challenge to the Catholic Church since the Roman persecutions of the third century. Led by a series of reform popes, the Church launched a Catholic Counter-Reformation to halt the spread of Protestantism and reenergize the faithful.

2. The Council of Trent reaffirmed that works of art should be employed to stimulate piety. Painters, sculptors, and architects tried to speak to the faithful by creating dramatic works of art that involved worshippers.

B. CHARACTERISTICS OF BAROQUE ART

1. Dramatic use of light and dark called tenebrism
2. Subject matter focused on dramatic moments
3. Portrayal of everyday people who are not idealized
4. Baroque buildings featuring grandiose scale and ornate decorations

C. KEY EXAMPLES OF ITALIAN BAROQUE ART

1. Gian Lorenzo Bernini, *Baldachino* inside Saint Peter's
2. Michelangelo de Caravaggio, *The Calling of Saint Matthew*
3. Artemisia Gentileschi, *Judith Slaying Holofernes*

III. THE WARS OF KING PHILIP II OF SPAIN

A. PHILIP'S EMPIRE

1. Emperor Charles V abdicated his many thrones in 1556. He left his territories in Austria, Bohemia, and Hungary to his brother Ferdinand.

2. Charles left his son Philip a vast empire that included Spain, Milan, Naples, the Netherlands, and the overseas empire in the Americas.

B. PHILIP'S GOALS

1. To advance Spanish power in Europe
2. To champion Catholicism in Europe
3. To defeat the Ottoman Turks in the eastern Mediterranean

C. BATTLE OF LEPANTO, 1571

1. A combined Spanish-Venetian fleet defeated the Turkish navy at Lepanto off the coast of Greece.
2. The victory enhanced Philip's prestige as a champion of Catholicism.

D. THE DEFEAT OF PHILIP: THE NETHERLANDS

1. When Philip succeeded to the throne, the Spanish Netherlands consisted of 17 largely Catholic provinces.
2. Philip threatened traditional liberties by imposing the Inquisition and dispatching troops to support it. Philip's ill-considered actions provoked riots against the Spanish authorities.
3. Philip responded to this challenge by sending 20,000 additional troops. Led by the ruthless Duke of Alva, the Spaniards levied new taxes and sentenced thousands to death.
4. Alva's brutal actions united the Netherlands against the Spanish. During the struggle, many showed their opposition to Spain by converting to Calvinism.
5. A new Spanish viceroy, the Duke of Parma, adopted more skillful tactics. By substituting diplomacy for force, Parma was able to induce the ten southern provinces to reaffirm their loyalty to Spain.
6. Led by the province of Holland, the Dutch in the seven northern provinces could not be won back. In 1581, they boldly declared their independence from Spain.
7. The war for control of the Netherlands continued until 1609. Under the terms of a truce, the 7 northern and now heavily Calvinist provinces gained their independence and were known as Dutch. The 10 Catholic southern provinces were known as the Spanish Netherlands.

E. THE DEFEAT OF PHILIP: ENGLAND

1. The English felt threatened by Philip's aggressive actions in the Netherlands.
2. Queen Elizabeth openly assisted the Dutch rebels with money and troops. She also encouraged English sea captains to raid Spanish treasure ships.
3. Outraged by Elizabeth's interference, Philip assembled a huge fleet known as the Spanish Armada to invade England. Philip hoped to depose Elizabeth and return England to Catholicism.
4. Harassed by fast English ships, the powerful but slow-moving Spanish Armada never reached England. Only 67 of the Armada's original 130 ships returned to Spain.

F. CONSEQUENCES OF PHILIP'S DEFEATS

1. Although still a formidable military power, Spain began a long period of political and economic decline.
2. Now independent, the Dutch began a golden age of commercial prosperity and artistic creativity.
3. As Spain's influence declined, England's power increased. The English were now free to develop their overseas trade and to colonize North America.

THE FRENCH WARS OF RELIGION

A. THE CATHOLICS

1. As we have seen (chapter 4), under the terms of the Concordat of Bologne (1516), Francis I recognized the supremacy of the papacy over a universal council. In return, French rulers gained the right to appoint all French bishops and abbots.
2. As a result of the Concordat of Bologne, the ruling Valois kings had no reason to support a revolt against Rome.

B. THE HUGUENOTS

1. Despite royal opposition, Calvinist ideas gained a strong foothold in France. By the 1560s, one-tenth of France's 18 million people had become Calvinists, also known as Huguenots.
2. Calvinism had special appeal to French nobles. By the 1560s, between two-fifths and one-half of the nobility had become Calvinists. For many nobles, Calvinism provided a means of expressing opposition to the Valois kings.

C. THE SAINT BARTHOLOMEW'S DAY MASSACRE, 1572

1. The growing strength of the Huguenots alarmed the French king Charles IX and his powerful mother Catherine de' Medici.
2. With Catherine's support, Catholics killed thousands of Huguenots gathered in Paris to celebrate the wedding of Margaret of Valois to the Huguenot leader Henry of Navarre. The violence quickly spread to the provinces, where as many as 20,000 Huguenots were killed.
3. The Saint Bartholomew's Day massacre ignited a bloody civil war between Catholics and Huguenots that continued for 15 years.

D. THE POLITIQUES

1. The civil war devastated French agriculture and commerce.
2. A small group of moderate Catholics and Huguenots realized that the disorder and destruction had to be stopped or France would collapse. Known as politiques, they supported a strong monarchy and official recognition of the Huguenots.
3. The death of Catherine de' Medici followed by the assassinations of the powerful Catholic Duke of Guise and King Henry III paved the way for the accession of Henry of Navarre, a leading politique who became Henry IV in 1589.

E. THE EDICT OF NANTES, 1598

1. Henry IV was the leader of the House of Bourbon and a Huguenot.

2. Many Catholics, including the people of Paris, still opposed Henry. Knowing that a majority of the French were Catholics, Henry chose to become a Catholic saying, "Paris is worth a mass."

3. In 1598, Henry issued the Edict of Nantes proclaiming the toleration of Calvinism and recognizing the rights of French Protestants.

4. Henry's decision to convert and issue the Edict of Nantes saved France and prepared the way for the resurgence of royal power in the seventeenth century.

Test Tip

Be sure that you can Identify the St. Bartholomew's Day massacre, define the term politiques, and explain the terms of the Edict of Nantes. One or more of these three key points have appeared on almost every APEURO exam.

V. THE THIRTY YEARS' WAR, 1618–1648

A. THE HOLY ROMAN EMPIRE IN 1600

1. The Holy Roman Empire included approximately 300 small principalities, duchies, and independent cities.

2. The Peace of Augsburg in 1555 (see Chapter 5) gave each German prince the right to determine the religion of his state, either Roman Catholic or Lutheran.

3. The Peace of Augsburg did not provide for the recognition of Calvinists. Nonetheless, a number of states, including the Palatinate, had adopted Calvinism.

B. CAUSES OF THE THIRTY YEARS' WAR

1. Religious divisions
   ▶ *In 1608, the Protestant states formed the Protestant Union to defend their interests.*
   ▶ *The following year the Catholic states formed the Catholic League to defend their interests.*

2. Political divisions
   ▸ *The Austrian Habsburgs wanted to reverse the Protestant gains while building a stronger monarchy.*
   ▸ *The German principalities and independent cities were jealous of their rights and resisted any attempt at centralization.*
3. International interference
   ▸ *France opposed any policy that would create a strong power in Germany. So, although France was a Catholic power, it allied itself with Protestant princes.*
   ▸ *The Lutheran kings of Denmark and Sweden were prepared to defend Protestant interests in the Holy Roman Empire.*

C. THE FOUR PHASES OF THE THIRTY YEARS' WAR

1. The Bohemian Phase, 1618–1625
   ▸ *The Thirty Years' War began as a religious civil war in Bohemia between the Catholic League led by Emperor Ferdinand II and the Protestant Union led by Frederick V.*
   ▸ *Emperor Ferdinand II's forces won a series of victories that left the Habsburgs and Catholics in control of Bohemia.*
2. The Danish Phase, 1625–1629
   ▸ *Supported by the Dutch and English, King Christian IV, the Lutheran ruler of Denmark, intervened to support the Protestants.*
   ▸ *Led by Albert of Wallenstein, the imperial armies crushed the Protestant forces.*
   ▸ *Flushed with victory, Emperor Ferdinand issued the Edict of Restitution restoring all Catholic properties lost to the Protestants since 1552.*
3. The Swedish Phase, 1630–1635
   ▸ *Alarmed by the Catholic victories, the Protestants, Dutch, and French turned for help to the Lutheran king of Sweden, Gustavus Adolphus.*
   ▸ *A charismatic ruler and brilliant military strategist, Gustavus Adolphus defeated Wallenstein and the imperial forces in a series of decisive battles.*

- ▸ *The Swedish victories prevented the Habsburgs from uniting the German states.*

4. The French Phase, 1635–1648
    - ▸ *The death of Gustavus Adolphus prompted France to intervene on the Protestant side.*
    - ▸ *French, Dutch, and Swedish armies burned German farms and destroyed German commerce.*

D. THE PEACE OF WESTPHALIA, 1648

1. The setting
    - ▸ *Hundreds of diplomats representing the German states, France, Sweden, Spain, the Dutch and the pope met in Westphalia.*
    - ▸ *Although represented at Westphalia, the pope's objections were largely ignored, underscoring the degree of secularization taking place in Europe.*

2. The provisions
    - ▸ *Each of the over 300 German states received the right to conduct diplomacy and make treaties.*
    - ▸ *Rulers were allowed to decide the religious faith in their territory. Calvinism was recognized as an acceptable faith.*
    - ▸ *The independence of the Dutch Republic and neutrality of Switzerland were formally recognized.*
    - ▸ *The French annexed part of Alsace.*
    - ▸ *Sweden received additional territory around the Baltic Sea.*

E. CONSEQUENCES OF THE THIRTY YEARS' WAR

1. For Germany
    - ▸ *The Thirty Years' War devastated the German economy and decimated its population. As many as one-third of the German-speaking people died from disease, famine, and combat.*
    - ▸ *Germany's long-term commercial growth suffered because the Treaty of Westphalia gave control of the mouth of the Rhine River to the Dutch.*

▶ The Thirty Years' War left Germany politically fragmented, thus delaying German unification for two centuries.

2. For France

▶ France achieved its primary goals of weakening the Habsburgs and keeping the Holy Roman Empire weak and divided.

▶ France emerged as the strongest power in Europe.

The Thirty Years' War is both complex and important. Do not become bogged down trying to memorize the four phases of the war. Thus far, Gustavus Adolphus is the only leader who has been the answer to a multiple-choice question. Instead, focus on the long-term consequences of the Thirty Years' War for Germany and France. Pay special attention to the decline of the Holy Roman Empire and to the factors that prevented the development of a unified German state.

The Age of Exploration and the Commercial Revolution

I. **FACTORS THAT ENCOURAGED EUROPEAN OVERSEAS EXPLORATION**

A. THE RENAISSANCE SPIRIT OF INDIVIDUALISM

1. The explorers embodied the same spirit of individualism and curiosity that characterized Renaissance artists and humanist scholars.
2. The renewed interest in ancient writings that inspired Renaissance artists also gave the explorers new knowledge about mathematics, astronomy, and geography.

B. THE SEARCH FOR SPICES AND PROFITS

1. The Crusades helped stimulate a growing demand for Indian pepper, Chinese ginger, and Malukan cloves and nutmeg.
2. By the fourteenth century, European demand for Asian spices and luxury items far exceeded the supply. Muslims and Venetians controlled trade routes to the East.
3. The new monarchs in Spain and Portugal wanted direct access to the lucrative Asian markets.

C. THE DESIRE TO CULTIVATE CASH CROPS

1. A strong and growing demand for sugar motivated Europeans to look for lands suitable for cultivating this prized cash crop.
2. Europeans hoped to find lands where they could establish sugar plantations.

D. THE DESIRE TO SPREAD CHRISTIANITY

1. The Crusades left a legacy of hostility between Christians and Muslims.
2. Led by Spain and Portugal, Europeans hoped to reconquer northern Africa from the Muslims.
3. Europeans believed they had a duty to spread Christianity.

E. THE ABILITY TO USE NEW TECHNOLOGY

1. The newly designed caravel had square sails for running before the wind and triangular sails for tacking into the wind.
2. The magnetic compass and the astrolabe enabled mariners to determine their location at sea.

II. PORTUGAL: EAST BY SEA TO AN EMPIRE OF SPICES

A. PRINCE HENRY THE NAVIGATOR (1394–1460)

1. Prince Henry organized voyages along the west coast of Africa.
2. By the time of Prince Henry's death in 1460, the Portuguese had established a series of trading posts along the West African coast. These posts did a thriving business in gold and slaves.

B. THE PORTUGUESE TRADING-POST EMPIRE

1. Key explorers
   ▸ *Bartholomew Diaz rounded the Cape of Good Hope and returned to Portugal in 1488.*
   ▸ *Vasco da Gama reached the Malabar coast of India in 1498 and returned to Portugal with a cargo of pepper and cinnamon worth 60 times the cost of the expedition.*
   ▸ *Pedro Cabral accidentally discovered Brazil in 1500 while sailing to India. He returned to Portugal with 300,000 pounds of spices.*

2. Commercial trading posts
   ▸ *The Portuguese did not attempt to conquer territories. Instead, they built fortified trading posts designed to control trade routes.*
   ▸ *The most important Portuguese trading posts were located at Goa on the Indian coast, at Malacca on the Malay peninsula, and at Macao on the southern coast of China.*

C. CONSEQUENCES

1. The Portuguese ended the Venetian and Muslim monopoly of trade with Asia.
2. The center of European commerce shifted from the Mediterranean Sea to the Atlantic Ocean.
3. The new sea routes reduced the importance of the Baltic Sea thus leading to the decline of the Hanseatic League.

III. SPAIN: WEST BY SEA TO A NEW WORLD

A. CHRISTOPHER COLUMBUS (1451–1506)

1. Although he believed he had reached Asia, Columbus had in fact discovered Caribbean islands that were part of a vast New World.
2. Columbus's voyages helped to propel Spain into the forefront of European exploration, conquest, and settlement.

B. THE SPANISH CONQUESTS

1. Hernando Cortes conquered the Aztec empire in Mexico (1519–1521).
2. Francisco Pizarro conquered the Inca empire in Peru (1532–1533).

C. SPANISH AMERICA

1. By the end of the sixteenth century, Spain possessed an American empire twenty times its own size.

2. The Aztecs and other indigenous peoples were converted to Christianity and became subjects of the Spanish king.

3. The king of Spain governed his American empire through a Council of the Indies in Spain and through viceroys in Mexico City and Lima, Peru.

IV. THE COLUMBIAN EXCHANGE

A. INTRODUCTION

1. The Age of Exploration—also called the Age of Discovery—involved more than just the search for gold, silver, and spices.

2. The new discoveries sparked an unprecedented global diffusion of agricultural products, animals, diseases, and human populations.

B. NEW WORLD TO OLD WORLD

1. Agricultural products: potatoes, maize, tomatoes, peanuts, tobacco, vanilla, and chocolate

2. Animals: turkeys

3. Diseases: syphilis

C. OLD WORLD TO NEW WORLD

1. Agricultural products: coffee, cane sugar, wheat, and rice

2. Animals: cows, horses, pigs, sheep, goats, and chickens

3. Diseases: smallpox, measles, and diphtheria

4. Human populations: European colonists and African slaves

D. CONSEQUENCES OF THE COLUMBIAN EXCHANGE

1. For the New World

   ▸ *European diseases decimated indigenous populations. Approximately 90 percent of the indigenous peoples of the Americas perished between 1492 and 1600.*

   ▸ *The introduction of the horse transformed the culture of the Plains Indians of North America.*

2. For Europe
- ▶ *The new crops revolutionized the European diet and helped feed a growing population.*
- ▶ *The new Caribbean sugar plantations along with the rich silver and gold mines in Peru brought an influx of wealth to Spain that helped trigger inflation.*
- ▶ *The wealth generated by New World colonies dramatically increased the power of western Europe.*

3. For Africa
- ▶ *The wealth produced by New World sugar and tobacco plantations promoted the triangular trading system and the trans-Atlantic slave trade.*
- ▶ *Between 1500 and 1800, Africans comprised the largest group of people transported to the New World.*

The Columbian exchange is generating an increasing number of questions on APEURO exams. Test writers are using multiple-choice questions to test your knowledge of the agricultural products, animals, diseases, and human populations involved in the exchange. They are using essay questions to test your knowledge of the effects of the Columbian exchange on Europe's population and economy.

V. THE COMMERCIAL REVOLUTION

A. CAUSES

1. New ocean trade routes
- ▶ *The trade in spices, sugar, and precious metals brought great wealth to the European trading nations.*
- ▶ *The wealth supported increased investment and a wide array of new economic ventures.*

2. Growth of population
- ▶ *The introduction of new foods played a key role in supporting population growth.*
- ▶ *The population of Europe increased from 70 million in 1500 to 90 million in 1600.*

> ▸ *The steady rise in population increased overall demand for goods and services.*

3. Price revolution
   > ▸ *During the sixteenth century, the western European economy experienced a steady inflation in prices.*
   > ▸ *The influx of gold and silver from the New World and the rising demand created by the growth of population contributed to the price revolution.*

4. New nation-centered economic system
   > ▸ *Prior to 1500, the western European economy was organized around towns and guilds. Both relied upon strict regulations to ensure their survival. As a result, there was very little innovation.*
   > ▸ *As commercial activity increased, a new nation-centered economic system began to replace the old town-and-guild framework.*

B. KEY FEATURES

1. New entrepreneurs
   > ▸ *The expansion of commercial activity created large geographic markets. The new trading areas opened new opportunities while also requiring a new kind of economic leadership.*
   > ▸ *As the commercial revolution replaced the town-and-guild framework, merchants and bankers emerged as influential and successful entrepreneurs.*
   > ▸ *The Italian Medici family and the German Fuggers were prominent examples of the new economic entrepreneurs.*

2. New industries
   > ▸ *The printing press created a national and even international market for books.*
   > ▸ *The new ocean trading routes sparked a rise in shipbuilding.*
   > ▸ *The emergence of nation-states supported the large-scale manufacture of cannons and muskets.*

3. New domestic or putting-out system
   > ▸ *Strict guild regulations stifled competition and restricted production.*

▸ *In order to avoid the restrictive guild system, entrepreneurs provided cloth, looms, and other equipment to rural families.*

▸ *The putting-out or domestic system led to a significant increase in the production of cloth and other manufactured goods.*

4. New joint-stock companies

▸ *The new international trade required unprecedented amounts of capital. For example, merchants had to arm their ships, buy special privileges for local authorities, and build trading posts. Wars, storms, and rivals all threatened profits.*

▸ *English and Dutch merchants formed joint-stock companies to maximize profits and limit risks.*

▸ *Investors in a joint-stock company bought shares of ownership. If the company went bankrupt, its owners lost their investment. If the companies prospered, the investor's shares of ownership entitled them to collect a proportional share of the profits.*

C. MERCANTILISM

1. The rulers of the new nation-states adopted a system of economic principles and policies called mercantilism.

2. Mercantilists wanted to build strong, self-sufficient economies.

3. According to mercantilist theory, colonies should export raw materials and import finished goods. This would create a favorable balance of trade and the resulting growth of national reserves of gold and silver.

Test Tip

Joint-stock companies and mercantilism are well-known economic terms that have generated a number of questions. Given the emphasis on these terms, it is easy to overlook the putting-out system. Don't make this mistake. Most APEURO exams contain a multiple-choice question designed to see if you understand the causes and consequences of the putting-out system.

D. CONSEQUENCES

1. Decline of early commercial centers
   ▶ *During the 1400s, a confederacy of Baltic towns known as the Hanseatic League dominated northern European trade. As the center of European trade shifted to the rising nation-states in western Europe, the Hanseatic League rapidly declined.*
   ▶ *Led by Venice, Italian city-states had controlled the lucrative trade with India. The Portuguese broke this monopoly by pioneering a new sea route to Asia.*

2. Rise of capitalism
   ▶ *Capitalism is an economic system in which capital, or wealth, is invested to produce more capital.*
   ▶ *Capitalism is based upon the private ownership of property such as land, raw materials, and equipment.*
   ▶ *Capitalists are motivated by a desire to earn profits.*
   ▶ *The Age of Discovery ushered in a new economic era dominated by commercial capitalism.*

3. Rise of the bourgeoisie
   ▶ *As commercial capitalism expanded so did the class of entrepreneurs. The new middle class is called the bourgeoisie.*
   ▶ *As commercial capitalism expanded, so did the wealth and power of the bourgeoisie.*

Constitutionalism: The Dutch Republic and England, 1600–1689

I. THE DUTCH REPUBLIC

A. POLITICAL INDEPENDENCE

1. Each of the seven Dutch provinces was politically independent.
2. Unlike the other continental nations, the Dutch were not governed by an absolute ruler.
3. Instead, political power passed into the hands of wealthy merchants.

B. RELIGIOUS TOLERATION

1. Calvinism was the dominant religion.
2. However, Catholics, Lutherans, Anabaptists, and Jews all enjoyed religious freedom.
3. This religious toleration helped create a cosmopolitan society that promoted commerce.

C. ECONOMIC PROSPERITY

1. The Dutch Republic was Europe's leading commercial power during most of the seventeenth century. Amsterdam remained Europe's financial center until the French Revolution.
2. Shipbuilding played a key role in the Dutch economy. The Dutch fleet of 10,000 ships was the largest in the world.
3. As trade routes shifted from the Mediterranean to the Atlantic, the Dutch replaced the Italians as the bankers of Europe. Founded in 1609, the Amsterdam Exchange Bank

quickly won a reputation as the safest, soundest bank in Europe.

4. The Dutch East Indies Company displaced the Portuguese and gained control of the lucrative spice trade in the East Indies.

D. ARTISTIC CREATIVITY

1. The Dutch Republic was a Protestant nation without an absolute ruler. This made the Dutch art very different from the baroque art in Rome and Madrid. Baroque artists working in these cities created works of art designed to glorify the Catholic Church and the ruling monarchs.

2. Lacking commissions from the Catholic Church and from royal officials, Dutch artists turned to their nation's prosperous merchants. As self-made entrepreneurs they wanted to purchase paintings of themselves, their families, their possessions, and their land.

3. Dutch artists focused on painting individual and group portraits, landscapes, and genre scenes of everyday life.

4. During the 1600s, the Dutch Republic supported an astonishing number of great artists. Led by Frans Hals, Rembrandt, and Jan Vermeer, the Dutch enjoyed a golden age of artistic achievement.

E. ECONOMIC DECLINE

1. Costly wars with England and France damaged the Dutch Republic.

2. As the Dutch Republic declined, England and France became the dominant European powers.

Test Tip

The Dutch Republic generates a number of very predictable questions. For example, almost every APEURO exam has had a question designed to see if you know that Amsterdam was Europe's leading commercial center during the seventeenth century. Also be sure that you know the unique characteristics and subjects of Dutch art.

II. ENGLISH SOCIETY IN THE SEVENTEENTH CENTURY

A. IMPACT OF THE COMMERCIAL REVOLUTION

1. As the commercial revolution gained momentum, the size of the English middle class increased.
2. With the exception of the Dutch Republic, the English middle class was proportionally larger than that of any country in Europe.
3. English entrepreneurs financed joint-stock companies that played a key role in promoting English colonies in North America.

B. GENTRY

1. The gentry included wealthy landowners who dominated the House of Commons.
2. It is very important to note that unlike France, the English gentry was willing to pay taxes. This had two important consequences:
   ▸ *First, since the tax burden was more equitable in England, the peasantry was not overburdened with excessive taxes.*
   ▸ *Second, the gentry and thus the House of Commons demanded a role in determining national expenditures. This created an inevitable conflict with the Stuart kings.*

C. RELIGION

1. By the end of the seventeenth century, Calvinists comprised the largest percentage of the English population.
2. Puritans continued to demand changes in the Anglican church.

 III. KEY ISSUES

A. THE ROLE OF THE MONARCH

1. The Stuart kings believed that their authority came from God.

CHRONOLOGICAL REVIEW

2. The Stuart kings thus wanted a monarchy free from parliamentary restraints.

B. THE ROLE OF THE HOUSE OF COMMONS

1. The House of Commons was dominated by the gentry, merchants, and lawyers.
2. Members were determined to preserve traditional privileges such as freedom of open debate and immunity from arrest.
3. They demanded a stronger voice in political affairs.

C. ORGANIZATION OF THE ANGLICAN CHURCH

1. The Stuarts favored the established Episcopal form of church organization. In this hierarchical arrangement, the king, Archbishop of Canterbury, and bishops determined doctrine and practice.
2. The Puritans favored a Presbyterian form of church organization. This arrangement allowed church members a much greater voice in running the church and expressing dissenting views.

 # IV. JAMES I (reigned 1603–1625)

A. DIVINE RIGHT OF KINGS

1. James believed that royal authority came directly from God.
2. James published a work called *The True Law of Free Monarchies* in which he asserted that "kings are not only God's lieutenants upon earth, and sit on God's throne, but even by God himself they are called gods."

B. QUARRELS WITH PARLIAMENT

1. Puritan members of Parliament urged James to "purify" the Church of England of "popish remnants" including the authority of bishops.
2. James was convinced that the Presbyterian system of church government would destroy royal control of the church

and threaten the monarchy. He reportedly summed up his opposition by declaring, "No bishops, no king."

V. CHARLES I (reigned 1625–1649) AND PARLIAMENT

A. LIKE FATHER, LIKE SON

1. Like his father, Charles I was a firm believer in the divine right of kings.
2. Like his father, Charles I was always in need of money.
3. And finally, like his father, Charles opposed the Puritans and supported the Anglican Church.

B. PETITION OF RIGHT, 1628

1. In return for grants of money, Charles I agreed to the Petition of Right.
2. The Petition of Right contained two key provisions:
   ▸ *No one should be compelled to pay any tax or loan "without common consent by act of Parliament."*
   ▸ *No one should be imprisoned without due process of law.*

C. RELIGIOUS POLICIES

1. Religion was the single most explosive issue in England.
2. With Charles's encouragement, William Laud, Archbishop of Canterbury, attempted to transform the Church of England into a Catholic church without a pope.
3. In 1639, Laud foolishly attempted to impose the English Prayer Book on the Scottish Presbyterian Church.
4. Determined to defend their religion, the Scots formed an army and occupied northern England.

D. THE LONG PARLIAMENT, 1640–1648

1. Desperate for money to fight the Scots, Charles reluctantly recalled Parliament into session, thus precipitating a constitutional and religious crisis.

2. Determined to undo what they saw as royal tyranny, the Long Parliament executed Laud and passed a number of laws limiting royal power.

Test Tip

The period from 1640 to 1660 can be very confusing. Don't spend your time memorizing the Short Parliament, the Long Parliament, and the Rump Parliament. Instead, focus on the causes and consequences of the changing relationship between the monarchy and Parliament.

VI. THE ENGLISH CIVIL WAR, 1642–1649

A. THE CAVALIERS

1. The Cavaliers were aristocrats, nobles, and church officials who remained loyal to the king.
2. Cavaliers favored a strong monarchy and an Anglican Church governed by bishops appointed by the crown.

B. THE ROUNDHEADS

1. The Roundheads included Puritans, townspeople, middle-class businessmen, and people from Presbyterian-dominated London.
2. Roundheads favored a Parliamentary monarchy and a Presbyterian church governed by elected "presbyters" or elders.

C. OLIVER CROMWELL

1. Led by Oliver Cromwell, a previously unknown country gentleman, the Roundheads defeated the Cavaliers.
2. Cromwell organized an army of zealous Protestants called the New Model Army.
3. In January 1649, Cromwell and his supporters executed King Charles I.

VII. **THE INTERREGNUM UNDER OLIVER CROMWELL**

A. THE COMMONWEALTH AND THE PROTECTORATE

1. With Charles I executed, Cromwell now held the reigns of power.
2. The Commonwealth (1649–1653) abolished the monarchy and the House of Lords. Oliver Cromwell and a one-house Parliament exercised political power.
3. In late 1653, Cromwell took the title Lord Protector, establishing a one-man rule supported by the army.

B. FOREIGN POLICY

1. Cromwell brutally crushed a royalist uprising in Ireland. Protestant landlords replaced Catholic property owners. Nearly half of Ireland's population may have perished from famine and plague.
2. England passed the Navigation Act of 1651. The act barred Dutch ships from carrying goods between other countries and England. The act was also designed to give England greater control over its American colonies.
3. England waged a series of wars that weakened the Dutch.

C. DOMESTIC POLICY

1. The Puritans attempted to impose a strict moral code that censored the press, prohibited sports, and closed theaters.
2. Cromwell opposed radical groups such as the Levellers and the Quakers.
   ▸ *The Levellers advocated a more egalitarian society with nearly universal manhood suffrage and a written constitution guaranteeing equal rights to all.*
   ▸ *The Quakers rejected religious hierarchies and allowed women to preach at their meetings.*

D. THE DEATH OF CROMWELL

1. Oliver Cromwell ruled until his death in 1658. His son Richard did not command the same respect as his father.

2. Parliament invited Prince Charles Stuart, the eldest son of Charles I to return from exile.

VIII. THE RESTORATION

A. CHARLES II (REIGNED 1660–1685)

1. The Restoration restored the monarchy, the Church of England, and Parliament.
2. Nonetheless, the central issues concerning the relationship between the king and Parliament and the conflict over religion remained unresolved.

B. THE QUESTION OF THE SUCCESSION

1. Charles's second wife and his brother, the Duke of York, were Roman Catholic.
2. Since Charles had no legitimate children, his brother James was next in line to the throne.

C. TORIES AND WHIGS

1. The debate over James's successor divided Parliament into two groups:
   - *The Whigs were deeply suspicious of Catholics and wanted to lawfully exclude James from the throne.*
   - *The Tories felt a strong loyalty to the monarchy and supported James's right to the throne.*
2. The Whigs and the Tories became the first political parties in the English-speaking world.

D. JAMES II (REIGNED 1685–1688)

1. Despite opposition from the Whigs, James II inherited the throne. He promptly adopted policies that antagonized both Whigs and Tories. Determined to return England to Catholicism, he appointed Catholics to influential positions of power.

2. James's second wife was a Catholic. In June 1688, she gave birth to a son who became the next heir to the throne.

IX. THE GLORIOUS REVOLUTION

A. WILLIAM AND MARY

1. James's first wife had been a Protestant who raised their eldest daughter, Mary, as a Protestant. Mary was the wife of William of Orange, a powerful Dutch leader.
2. Whigs and Tories invited William and Mary to overthrow James II for the sake of Protestantism. Faced with united opposition, James II fled to France.

B. THE BILL OF RIGHTS, 1689

1. In 1689, Parliament required William and Mary to accept a Bill of Rights.
2. The Bill of Rights contained the following key provisions:
   - *The members of Parliament enjoyed the right to free debate.*
   - *Taxation required parliamentary consent.*
   - *Laws could be made only with the consent of Parliament.*
   - *The monarch could not be a Roman Catholic.*
   - *Parliament would hold frequent sessions.*
   - *Parliament could be dissolved only by its own consent.*
   - *No subject could be arrested and detained without legal consent.*

C. IMPORTANCE

1. The English rejected the theory of the divine right of kings.
2. The Glorious Revolution—as the overthrow of James II in favor of William and Mary came to be known—placed clear limits on the power of the English monarchy.
3. England became a constitutional monarchy controlled by an aristocratic oligarchy.

X. MAKING COMPARISONS: HOBBES AND LOCKE

A. THOMAS HOBBES (1588–1679)

1. Background
   - ▸ *Hobbes published* Leviathan *in 1651, just two years after the execution of Charles I.*
   - ▸ *The horrors of the English civil war left a deep impression on Hobbes.*

2. Beliefs on human nature
   - ▸ *Human beings are naturally self-centered and prone to violence.*
   - ▸ *Human beings are motivated to increase pleasure and minimize pain. They engage in a "perpetual and restless desire" for power.*

3. Beliefs on the state of nature
   - ▸ *In a state of nature, people know neither peace nor security.*
   - ▸ *In a state of nature, life is "solitary, poor, nasty, brutish, and short."*

4. Arguments for a strong government
   - ▸ *Without government, life would be intolerable and civilization impossible.*
   - ▸ *Government is the result of human necessity rather than divine ordination.*
   - ▸ *People give up their personal liberty to attain security and order.*
   - ▸ *Fearing the dangers of anarchy more than tyranny, Hobbes argued that rulers should have absolute and unlimited political authority.*

B. JOHN LOCKE (1632–1704)

1. Background
   - ▸ *Locke published* Second Treatise of Government *in 1690.*
   - ▸ *Locke presented a compelling argument that justified the Glorious Revolution and later inspired Thomas Jefferson when he wrote the Declaration of Independence.*

2. Beliefs on human nature
   ▸ *Locke rejected the Hobbesian view that humans are innately brutish. People are instead the products of their training, education, and experience.*
   ▸ *Locke viewed humans as creatures of reason and goodwill.*

3. Locke's "law of nature"
   ▸ *Locke formulated the theory of "natural rights."*
   ▸ *He argued that people are born with basic rights to "life, liberty, and property."*
   ▸ *These rights are derived from what Locke called the "law of nature," which existed before the creation of government.*

4. Arguments for limited government
   ▸ *People form governments to preserve their natural rights.*
   ▸ *Government is a contract in which the rulers promise to safeguard the people's natural rights.*
   ▸ *If rulers betray their trust, the governed have the right to replace them.*

Absolutism in Western Europe: France and Spain, 1589–1715

I. FOUNDATIONS OF ABSOLUTISM IN FRANCE, 1589–1661

A. HENRY IV

1. The Edict of Nantes, 1598
   - *The edict granted religious toleration to the French Huguenots.*
   - *It established Henry IV as a politique who placed political expediency above religious principles.*
2. The Duke de Sully and financial reform
   - *The French tax system was both inefficient and inequitable. Nobles were exempt from paying taxes. As a result, the burden fell most heavily upon the peasants.*
   - *Henry appointed the Duke de Sully as his chief minister. Sully could not make the tax system more just. But he did make it more efficient. His policies reduced the royal debt, built new roads and canals, revived industry and agriculture, and encouraged colonization in the New World.*
3. The nobility of the robe
   - *The nobles posed the greatest threat to the extension of royal power. The influence of this "nobility of the sword" was based upon inherited privileges and a tradition of military service.*

▶ *Henry IV and Sully began the process of raising revenue by selling government offices that conferred nobility. Known as robe nobles, these new nobles were members of the increasingly prosperous bourgeoisie.*

B. LOUIS XIII AND CARDINAL RICHELIEU

1. The rise of Richelieu

▶ *Henry IV was assassinated in 1610, leaving his nine-year-old son Louis XIII (reigned 1610–1643) as the second Bourbon monarch.*

▶ *In 1624, Louis appointed Cardinal Richelieu to be his chief minister. Richelieu was the real ruler of France from 1624 until his death in 1642.*

▶ *Richelieu worked tirelessly and successfully to enhance royal power. Like Henry IV, Richelieu was a politique who placed public order above religious zeal.*

2. The intendant system

▶ *Richelieu was determined to weaken the nobility.*

▶ *At that time, France was divided into thirty-two administrative districts. Richelieu replaced nobles with royal officials called intendants. The intendants implemented royal orders.*

▶ *The intendants were typically middle-class or minor nobles drawn from the nobility of the robe.*

▶ *The intendant system played an important role in strengthening royal power.*

▶ *It is important to note that while the intendant system curbed the nobles' political power, it did not lessen their economic or social privileges.*

3. International affairs

▶ *Richelieu continued France's long-term policy of limiting Habsburg power.*

▶ *Richelieu supported the Protestant powers during the Thirty Years' War. His skillful diplomacy and well-timed interventions helped defeat the Habsburgs and make France the leading European power.*

C. THE FRONDE

1. The deaths of Richelieu in 1642 and Louis XIII the following year left the monarchy in the hands of the five-year-old Louis XIV and his chief minister, Cardinal Mazarin.

2. Sensing royal weakness, the nobles led a series of rebellions against royal authority. Known as the Fronde, these rebellions were intended to limit rather than overthrow the monarchy.

3. Increasing violence and instability forced the young king, Louis XIV, to flee Paris. Louis remembered this humiliation and vowed to control the nobility.

Both the intendant system and the Fronde generate a significant number of multiple-choice questions on the APEURO exam. The intendant system was designed to strengthen royal authority while the Fronde was intended to weaken the king's power. The Fronde played a key role in prompting Louis XIV to move to Versailles.

II. LOUIS XIV, THE SUN KING

A. BISHOP BOSSUET AND THE DIVINE RIGHT OF KINGS

1. Bishop Bossuet was a prominent French churchman, a renowned orator, and the principal theorist of the seventeenth-century doctrine of absolutism.

2. Bossuet argued that all power comes from God. The king inherited his position and authority from God.

3. Royal power was absolute. Subjects must obey their sovereign as the direct representative of God on earth.

4. While royal power was absolute, it was not arbitrary. Monarchs had to obey God's laws and were responsible to God for their conduct.

B. "I AM THE STATE."

1. Louis XIV was the most powerful monarch in French history. Unlike the English monarchs, Louis did not share his power

with a parliament. In Louis's view, he and the nation were the same. He reportedly boasted, *"L'etat, c'est moi,"* meaning "I am the state."

2. Louis increased the powers of the intendants, refused to appoint a chief minister, and regularly attended meetings of his four great councils.

3. Louis continued Richelieu's policy of reducing the political power of the French nobility. He excluded nobles from key positions and instead appointed men from bourgeoisie and recently ennobled families.

C. THE VERSAILLES PALACE

1. As an absolute monarch, Louis XIV determined foreign policy, commanded the army, and supported the arts. His description of himself as the "Sun King" was accurate. In France, all aspects of political life and culture revolved around Louis XIV.

2. Louis XIV understood the power of art as propaganda and the value of visual imagery for cultivating a public image. The Versailles Palace was designed to be a visible symbol of Louis XIV's absolute power and greatness.

3. The Versailles Palace underscored France's cultural dominance. French art, philosophy, architecture, and fashions were envied and copied throughout the continent.

D. COLBERT AND MERCANTILISM

1. Louis XIV named Jean-Baptiste Colbert as controller general of finances. Colbert worked tirelessly to strengthen France's economy by implementing strict mercantilist policies.

2. Colbert expanded manufacturing by abolishing domestic tariffs that inhibited trade. At the same time, he protected French products by placing high tariffs on goods coming into the country.

3. Colbert recognized the importance of colonies as a source of raw materials and a market for manufactured goods. He encouraged people to emigrate to Canada where the lucrative fur trade promoted French commerce.

4. Colbert was able to raise royal revenues and promote economic growth. However, he was unable to make the tax system more equitable. Nobles continued to enjoy exemptions while peasants continued to bear a disproportionate tax burden.

E. REVOCATION OF THE EDICT OF NANTES

1. When Louis XIV's reign began, France's population of 19 million people included about a million Huguenots. The Huguenots continued to enjoy religious toleration and had remained loyal to the crown during the Fronde.

2. Louis's goal of having "one king, one law, one faith" precluded religious diversity. Supported by the French Catholic clergy and his Jesuit advisors, Louis revoked the Edict of Nantes in 1685. Royal officials closed Protestant churches and ordered all Protestant children baptized as Catholics.

3. Louis XIV paid a high price for his religious intolerance. To escape persecution, some 200,000 Huguenots fled to England, the Dutch Republic, Protestant German states, and the New World. As a result, France lost many skilled workers and business leaders.

III. THE WARS OF LOUIS XIV

A. STRATEGIC GOALS

1. France was the most powerful and populous nation in Europe.

2. Louis XIV had two strategic goals:
   ▸ *First, he wanted France to expand to its "natural frontiers" along the Rhine River and Switzerland.*
   ▸ *Second, he wanted to make France a global power by inheriting the Spanish Habsburg possessions in the New World and in Europe.*

B. THE BALANCE OF POWER

1. Louis XIV's powerful army and ambitious plans threatened to create a "universal monarchy" in which other nations would be subordinated to France's political will.

2. Alone, no European country was a match for France. However, by joining together, weaker countries could equal or even exceed French power. This defensive strategy is known as a balance of power. In such a balance, no one country can dominate the others.

3. Louis repeatedly sent French armies into the Netherlands in an attempt to extend his boundaries to the Rhine River. Each time, a coalition formed by the Dutch Republic thwarted him.

C. THE WAR OF THE SPANISH SUCCESSION, 1701–1713

1. In 1700, the balance of power was once again threatened when the childless king of Spain, Charles II, died. In his will, the dying king bequeathed the Spanish throne and its huge overseas empire to Louis's 17-year-old grandson, Philip of Anjou.

2. The nations of Europe feared that Louis could now create a universal monarchy that would upset the balance of power. Led by England, they formed a Grand Alliance that included Holland, Austria, Brandenburg, and the Italian duchy of Savoy.

3. The War of the Spanish Succession proved to be a costly struggle that left France battered and weakened. The war's huge debts played a key role in worsening financial and social tensions that would later erupt in the French Revolution.

D. THE TREATY OF UTRECHT, 1713

1. The Treaty of Utrecht created a new balance of power that preserved the peace for 30 years.

2. French gains
   ▸ *Louis's grandson, Philip V, was allowed to remain king of Spain as long as the thrones of Spain and France were not united.*
   ▸ *France was allowed to retain all of Alsace.*

3. English gains
   ▶ *England gained valuable Spanish naval bases at Gibraltar and in the Balearic Islands.*
   ▶ *England gained the asiento (slave trade) from Spain.*
   ▶ *England gained valuable French colonies in Nova Scotia and Newfoundland.*
4. Austrian gains
   ▶ *Austria gained the Spanish Netherlands (Belgium), which then became known as the Austrian Netherlands.*
   ▶ *Austria obtained Naples, Milan, and Sardinia.*
5. The Duke of Savoy
   ▶ *As a reward for joining the Grand Alliance, the Duke of Savoy received Sicily and the title of king.*
   ▶ *In 1720, Savoy ceded Sicily to Austria in exchange for Sardinia.*
6. The Elector of Brandenburg
   ▶ *As a reward for joining the Grand Alliance, the Elector of Brandenburg was recognized as king of Prussia.*

Don't spend time studying Louis XIV's many wars. Instead, focus on the consequences of these wars and the provisions of the Treaty of Utrecht. It is important to note that the Spanish Netherlands (Belgium) became the Austrian Netherlands. Also note the emerging role of the rulers of Savoy and Brandenburg.

IV. THE DECLINE OF SPANISH POWER

A. THE GOLDEN AGE OF SPAIN

1. Ferdinand and Isabella built the foundation of Spanish absolutism.
2. Spanish power reached its zenith during the reign of Philip II (reigned 1556–1598).
3. Spanish power and prestige began to steadily decline during the seventeenth century.

B. ECONOMIC DECLINE

1. The expulsion of Jews and converted Muslims, known as Moriscos, deprived Spain of prosperous merchants and skilled workers.

2. The flow of gold and silver from Mexico and Peru proved to be a mixed blessing. At first, the precious metals enriched the Spanish economy. However, the flood of imported silver also caused inflation, which increased the cost of Spanish textiles and other products. As a result, Spanish exports declined.

3. A series of costly wars with the Dutch Republic and France extended Spain's commitments beyond the nation's declining resources.

4. Spanish industry, commerce, agriculture, and population all declined.

C. POLITICAL DECLINE

1. Spain suffered from a series of weak and inept rulers who pursued misguided and ineffective policies.

2. Spanish rulers and aristocrats continued to lead extravagant lifestyles they could no longer afford.

3. Spanish armies suffered a series of disastrous defeats.

V. MAKING COMPARISONS: THE ECONOMIC DECLINE OF THE DUTCH REPUBLIC AND SPAIN

A. GREATNESS AND PROSPERITY

1. In the sixteenth century, Spain conquered and then developed a world colonial empire. The sixteenth century was a period of Spanish greatness and prosperity.

2. In the seventeenth century, the Dutch Republic developed a commercial empire, becoming a center of international finance. The seventeenth century was a period of Dutch greatness and prosperity.

3. Nonetheless, by 1713, both Spain and the Dutch Republic were second-rate powers that were eclipsed by France and England.

B. FACTORS RESPONSIBLE FOR ECONOMIC DECLINE

1. The high costs of war

   ▸ *A series of costly wars severely damaged Spain's economy. Spain fought lengthy wars with both the Dutch Republic and France.*

   ▸ *The economy of the Dutch Republic also suffered from costly wars. In 1670, both France and England attacked the Dutch Republic. The French army occupied a substantial part of the country, forcing the Dutch to open their dikes to save Amsterdam. Led by William III, the Dutch played a key role in helping defeat France in the War of the Spanish Succession.*

2. Economic competition

   ▸ *Both the French and the English cast covetous eyes on Spain's New World possessions.*

   ▸ *The enormous costs of fighting France for 40 years eroded the Dutch Republic's competitive edge. In addition, the Dutch faced increasing economic competition from England.*

3. Small populations

   ▸ *Spain's population shrank from approximately 7.5 million in 1550 to 5.5 million in 1660. A declining population reduced the domestic demand for Spanish goods.*

   ▸ *The Dutch Republic's population increased from 1.5 million in 1600 to just under 2 million in 1700. Nonetheless, this population was too small to maintain and defend a global commercial empire.*

Absolutism in Eastern Europe, 1600–1725

I. THREE DECLINING EMPIRES

A. EASTERN EUROPE IN 1648

1. The Holy Roman Empire, the Republic of Poland, and the Ottoman Empire occupied the area from the French border to Russia.
2. All three empires were declining. Each lacked a strong central authority and efficient systems of government.
3. Each of the declining empires contained diverse ethnic and language groups.

B. THE HOLY ROMAN EMPIRE

1. The Reformation left the Holy Roman Empire religiously divided between Catholics and Protestants.
2. The Thirty Years' War left the Holy Roman Empire politically divided into 300 independent states.
3. The empire had an elected emperor who had no imperial army, revenues, or centralized authority.
4. Led by the Habsburgs and the Hohenzollerns, Austria and Prussia gradually emerged as the leading German states.

C. THE REPUBLIC OF POLAND

1. On a map of Europe in 1660, Poland appears to be a large, united country. In reality, the king of Poland was elected by Polish nobles who severely restricted his power.
2. Poland did have a central diet. However, action required the unanimous consent of each aristocratic member. Any

member could break up or "explode" the diet by objecting to a policy or act.

3. Poland's lack of centralized power created a power vacuum that left it vulnerable to stronger and more aggressive nations.

D. THE OTTOMAN EMPIRE

1. Led by Suleiman the Magnificent (reigned 1520–1566), the Ottomans threatened Vienna.
2. In the middle of the seventeenth century, a series of ambitious rulers revitalized the Ottoman Empire. In 1683, a powerful Turkish army once again besieged Vienna.
3. Austrian forces reinforced by Poles and Germans successfully repelled the Turks. This marked the beginning of a steady decline in Ottoman power.

II. THE HABSBURGS

A. THE REVIVAL OF HABSBURG POWER

1. The Habsburgs were one of the oldest dynasties in Europe. Beginning in the early 1400s, most of the Holy Roman emperors were Habsburgs.
2. Habsburg power suffered a series of setbacks following the devastation of the Thirty Years' War and the extinction of the Habsburg line in Spain.
3. Despite these defeats, the Habsburg rulers successfully reaffirmed their power over Austria, Bohemia, and Hungary. In addition, the Treaty of Utrecht gave the Habsburgs control of Naples, Sardinia, and Milan in Italy and the Spanish Netherlands (subsequently renamed the Austrian Netherlands).
4. It is important to note that the Habsburg empire embraced a large number of ethnic groups who were unified only by their Catholic faith and their loyalty to the Habsburg dynasty.

B. CHARLES VI AND THE PRAGMATIC SANCTION

1. Emperor Charles VI (reigned 1711–1740) did not have a male heir.

2. Determined to insure a safe succession for his daughter, Maria Theresa, Charles drew up a document called the Pragmatic Sanction. It stated that the territories of the Habsburg empire were indivisible and that Maria Theresa would inherit the throne and all Habsburg lands.

3. England and other foreign powers forced Charles to make a number of concessions before agreeing to the Pragmatic Sanction. Charles died believing he had guaranteed the peace and integrity of his realm.

Be sure that you can identify the Pragmatic Sanction. Charles VI devoted a significant part of his reign to winning European approval for this agreement. You should devote a few moments of study time to understanding the purpose of the Pragmatic Sanction. As you will see in chapter 12, Frederick the Great promptly violated the agreement by attacking Silesia.

III. THE RISE OF PRUSSIA

A. THE HOHENZOLLERNS OF BRANDENBURG-PRUSSIA

1. Brandenburg was a small state located between the Oder and Elbe rivers with its center in Berlin.

2. The ruler of Brandenburg was one of seven princes who elected the Holy Roman emperor.

3. The Hohenzollern family became the hereditary rulers of Brandenburg in 1417.

4. In the early seventeenth century, the Hohenzollerns inherited Cleves and some neighboring lands on the Rhine River and the duchy of Prussia on the Baltic coast to the northeast.

5. These diverse and geographically separated Hohenzollern possessions had no natural boundaries, few resources, and a population of just 1.5 million people.

B. FREDERICK WILLIAM, THE GREAT ELECTOR (REIGNED 1640–1688)

1. Although scattered and weak, the Hohenzollern possessions were the second-largest block of territory in the Holy Roman Empire. Only the Habsburgs could claim more land.

2. Known as the Great Elector, Frederick William began the process of forging the Hohenzollern territories into a strong power. He recognized that a well-equipped army would protect his territories and enable him to play a role in European balance-of-power politics.

3. Frederick William demanded and received the loyalty of the Junkers, the German landowners. In exchange, the Junkers received full power over the serfs who labored on their estates.

C. FREDERICK WILLIAM I (REIGNED 1713–1740)

1. Like the Great Elector, Frederick William I was determined to build a powerful army. During his reign, the Prussian military doubled to over 80,000 men. Although Prussia had Europe's thirteenth-largest population, it boasted the continent's third- or fourth-largest army.

2. Under the Hohenzollerns, military priorities and values dominated all aspects of Prussian life. Led by the Junkers, the officer corps became Prussia's most prestigious class. As noted by one foreign diplomat, "Prussia is not a state that possesses an army, but an army that possesses a state."

IV. RUSSIA BEFORE PETER THE GREAT

A. ISOLATION

1. Russia was geographically isolated from the rest of Europe. Sweden prevented Russia from reaching the Baltic Sea while the Ottoman Empire prevented Russia from reaching the Black Sea.

2. Russia was culturally isolated from the rest of Europe. The ideas of the Renaissance and Reformation and all the

discoveries of the Age of Exploration and the Scientific Revolution scarcely affected Russia.

B. THE ROMANOV DYNASTY

1. Following the death of Ivan the Terrible in 1584, Russia experienced a period of weakness and disorder known as the Time of Troubles.

2. Hoping to restore order, an assembly of nobles elected Michael Romanov to be the next czar. The Romanov Dynasty ruled Russia from 1613 to 1917.

V. PETER THE GREAT (reigned 1682–1725)

A. MODERNIZING RUSSIA

1. Peter the Great recognized that Russia had fallen behind western Europe. Determined to learn from his rivals, Peter visited Holland and England, where he toured shipyards, examined new military equipment, and observed western customs.

2. Peter returned to Moscow vowing to transform Russia into a great power. He began by expanding Russia's army and constructing a new navy.

3. Peter did not limit his changes to military organization and technology. He improved Russian agriculture by introducing the potato, strengthened the Russian economy by importing skilled workers, and liberated Russian women by allowing them to appear in public without veils. In a famous and much resented act, Peter forced nobles to shave off their traditional long beards.

B. DEFEATING SWEDEN

1. The Thirty Years' War left Sweden in control of the Baltic's entire eastern shore.

2. In 1700, Peter ordered his army to end Sweden's dominance of the Baltic. The Great Northern War between Sweden and Russia lasted from 1700 to 1721.

3. After suffering initial defeats at the hands of Sweden's king Charles XII, Peter ultimately won the war, thus gaining control over warm-water outlets on the Baltic shore.

4. The defeat contributed to Sweden's decline as a major European power. At the same time, Russia now became the dominant power on the Baltic Sea.

C. BUILDING ST. PETERSBURG

1. Peter the Great began building St. Petersburg in 1703. Named after his patron saint, St. Petersburg would be "a great window for Russia to look out at Europe."

2. St. Petersburg quickly became a symbol of Peter the Great's new and more powerful Russia.

D. CONTROLLING THE BOYARS

1. The boyars were the old nobility who supported traditional Russian culture.

2. Peter the Great did more than order the boyars to shave off their long beards and wear Western clothing. He also compelled them to construct costly town houses in St. Petersburg and required every noble to serve in the army or in the civil administration.

E. EXPLOITING THE SERFS

1. Russia's peasants did not enjoy the benefits of Peter the Great's reforms. Instead, they were conscripted into Russia's army and forced to build St. Petersburg.

2. In central Europe, serfs were bound to the land. In contrast, Russian serfs could be sold apart from the land. This enabled nobles to force serfs to work in mines and factories.

F. EVALUATING PETER THE GREAT

1. Peter the Great provided a model of how an energetic and ruthless autocrat would change a nation. He successfully transformed Russia into a great power that would play an increasingly important role in European history.

2. Peter the Great's policies increased the disparities between the nobles and the peasants. Millions of exploited serfs formed an estranged class that did not share in Russian society.

Peter the Great's momentous reign has been the subject of numerous multiple-choice questions and free-response essays on the APEURO exam. Peter the Great's successes include his program of modernization, construction of St. Petersburg, and victory over Sweden in the Great Northern War. However, Russia's economy continued to rest on the exploitation of serfs.

The Scientific Revolution and the Enlightenment

I. THE GEOCENTRIC VIEW OF THE UNIVERSE

A. OLD ASSUMPTIONS

1. Medieval philosophers accepted a geocentric view that held that the earth was a motionless body located at the center of the universe. The sun, moon, and planets all moved around the earth in perfectly circular paths.
2. Medieval philosophers believed that different physical laws applied to the earth and to the heavens.

B. TRADITIONAL AUTHORITIES

1. Both the Greek philosopher Aristotle and the Alexandrian astronomer Ptolemy supported the geocentric theory.
2. The Church taught that God had deliberately placed the earth at the center of the universe. Earth was thus a special place on which the great drama of life took place.

II. THE HELIOCENTRIC VIEW OF THE UNIVERSE

A. NICOLAUS COPERNICUS (1473–1543)

1. Copernicus was a Polish clergyman and astronomer. In his landmark book, *On the Revolutions of the Heavenly Bodies*, Copernicus directly challenged the geocentric view of the universe.
2. Copernicus presented his readers with a heliocentric view in which the earth revolved around the sun, which was the center of the universe.

B. JOHANNES KEPLER (1571–1630)

1. Copernicus's bold but controversial ideas were based on logic, not on direct observation. In the late 1500s, a Danish astronomer, Tycho Brahe, carefully recorded the movements of each known planet. When Brahe died in 1601, his assistant Johannes Kepler continued his work.

2 After carefully studying Brahe's data, Kepler formulated three laws of planetary motion:

  ▸ *The planets revolve around the sun in elliptical orbits.*
  ▸ *Planets move more rapidly as their orbits approach the sun.*
  ▸ *The time a planet takes to orbit the sun varies proportionately with its distance from the sun.*

C. GALILEO GALILEI (1564–1642)

1. Galileo was an Italian scientist who used controlled experiments to formulate laws of motion and inertia that were expressed in mathematical formulas.

2. Galileo was one of the first people to use the telescope for astronomical observation. His discoveries provided irrefutable support for the heliocentric view that the earth was a planet circling the sun.

3. Pope Urban VII accused Galileo of meddling "with the most important and dangerous subjects which can be stirred up in these days." In 1633, the pope summoned Galileo to Rome to stand trial. Under threat of torture, Galileo retracted his support for the Copernican theory.

III. THE SCIENTIFIC METHOD

A. SIR FRANCIS BACON (1561–1626) AND THE INDUCTIVE METHOD

1. Bacon contributed to scientific developments in the seventeenth century by advocating an inductive method for scientific experimentation.

2. The inductive method begins with direct observation of phenomena. This produces data that is systematically recorded and organized. The data leads to a tentative hypothesis that is retested in additional experiments.

3. Bacon argued that this process of controlled experimentation would lead to the formulation of universal principles and scientific laws.

B. RENE DESCARTES (1596–1650) AND THE DEVELOPMENT OF THE DEDUCTIVE METHOD

1. Descartes contributed to scientific developments in the seventeenth century by advocating a deductive method for the search for truth.

2. Descartes began by doubting all notions based on authority or custom. Instead, he started with a self-evident axiom known to be true. He then used logical reasoning to deduce various inferences.

C. CHARACTERISTICS OF THE SCIENTIFIC METHOD

1. Bacon's inductive method and Descartes deductive method proved to be complementary parts of a systematic and logical way of seeking truth known as the scientific method.

2. The scientific method includes the following characteristics:
   ‣ *Belief in the existence of regular patterns in nature*
   ‣ *Use of controlled experiments to systematically record facts and verify hypotheses*
   ‣ *Search for mathematical formulas to describe natural phenomena*

D. SCIENTIFIC SOCIETIES

1. Sponsored by governments and monarchs, scientists organized societies to promote research and spread scientific knowledge.

2. Founded in 1660, the Royal Society in England enjoyed international prestige. Other scientific societies were founded in Florence, Paris, and Berlin.

3. The scientific societies helped create an international scientific community.

IV. SIR ISAAC NEWTON (1642–1727)

A. NEWTON AND THE LAW OF GRAVITATION

1. Newton published the *Principia* in 1687. This momentous work combined Kepler's laws of planetary motion, Galileo's laws of inertia and falling bodies, and Newton's own conception of gravitation into a single mathematical law of universal gravitation.

2. Newton's concise mathematical formula described all forms of celestial and terrestrial motion.

B. THE NEWTONIAN UNIVERSE

1. Newton demonstrated that the universe is governed by universal laws that can be expressed in mathematical formulas.

2. Newton viewed the universe as a vast machine, created by God but working according to universal laws that could be discovered, mastered, and utilized to improve human life.

3. Supernatural and miraculous forces played no role in Newton's universe.

4. Newton's mechanistic concept of the universe dominated Western thought until the discoveries of Albert Einstein in the early twentieth century.

The Scientific Revolution is one of the watershed events in European intellectual history. APEURO test writers do not expect you to memorize scientific laws or mathematical formulas. They do expect you to discuss how pivotal figures such as Galileo, Bacon, Descartes, and Newton adopted a new view of nature that challenged long-held views of the relationship between humanity and the universe.

V. THE ENLIGHTENMENT

A. THE PHILOSOPHES

1. The philosophes were a group of thinkers and writers who espoused enlightened ideas. Taken together, they formed a grand "republic of letters."
2. The philosophes were not abstract philosophers. Instead, they dedicated themselves to exposing social problems and proposing reforms based upon implementing natural laws.
3. Although many leading philosophes were French, they were a cosmopolitan group who could be found in the American colonies and across Europe.

B. KEY IDEAS

1. Reason
   - *To the philosophes, reason was the absence of intolerance, bigotry, and superstition. Reason meant informed thinking about social problems.*
   - *Humans should rely on reason, not miracles, to improve society.*
2. Nature and natural laws
   - *The philosophes believed that natural laws regulate both the universe and human society.*
   - *These natural laws can be discovered by human reason.*
3. Happiness
   - *Philosophes had little interest in the medieval belief that people should accept misery in this world to find salvation in the hereafter.*
   - *Philosophes believed that happiness in this world was an inalienable human right.*
4. Progress
   - *The philosophes were the first Europeans to believe in social progress.*
   - *The discovery of laws of economics and government would improve society and make progress inevitable.*

5. Liberty

  ▸ *The philosophes lived in societies that placed restrictions on speech, religion, and trade. They wanted to remove these limitations on human liberty.*

  ▸ *The philosophes believed that intellectual freedom was a natural right. Without freedom of expression there could be no progress.*

6. Toleration

  ▸ *The philosophes questioned institutional religious beliefs, arguing that they perpetuated superstition, intolerance, and bigotry.*

  ▸ *The philosophes advocated full religious tolerance.*

C. DEISM

1. Deists thought of God as a cosmic watchmaker who created the universe and then let it run according to immutable natural laws.

2. Much of the educated elite in western Europe and America embraced deism. However, deism's reliance upon reason and its lack of emotion had little appeal for many people.

3. A new religious movement known as pietism stressed faith, emotion, and "the religion of the heart."

VI. VOLTAIRE (1694–1778)

A. PRINCE OF THE PHILOSOPHES

1. Voltaire was the best known and most influential philosophe.

2. He was a prolific writer who popularized Newton's scientific discoveries, criticized France's rigid government, and denounced religious bigotry.

B. "CRUSH THE INFAMOUS THING"

1. Voltaire directed his most stinging barbs at the intolerance of organized Christianity, both Protestant and Catholic.

2. Voltaire championed religious tolerance. He often ended his letters with the passionate demand to *"ecrasez l'infame"* ("crush the infamous thing"). This ringing exclamation reminded his readers to continue the battle against the enemies of reason—bigotry, ignorance, and religious fanaticism.

 DENIS DIDEROT (1713–1784) AND THE ENCYCLOPEDIA

A. PURPOSE

1. Diderot was a French philosophe who became the chief editor of the *Encyclopedia*.
2. Diderot's goal was to bring together all the most current and enlightened thinking about science, technology, mathematics, art, and government. "All things," Diderot explained, "must be examined, debated, investigated without exception and without regard for anyone's feelings."

B. IMPORTANCE

1. The *Encyclopedia* disseminated enlightened thinking across Europe and North America.
2. It undermined established authority by including articles about controversial political and religious subjects.

 BARON de MONTESQUIEU (1689–1755)

A. *THE SPIRIT OF THE LAWS*

1. Montesquieu was a French nobleman and attorney who wanted to limit the abuses of royal absolutism.
2. *The Spirit of the Laws* represented an attempt to create a "social science" by applying the methods of the natural sciences to the study of government.

B. SEPARATION OF POWERS

1. Montesquieu concluded that the ideal government separated powers among executive, legislative, and judicial branches.
2. This system of divided authority would protect the rights of individuals by preventing one branch of government from gaining unrestricted control over the entire society.
3. Montesquieu's ideas had a significant influence on the writers of the American Constitution.

IX. JEAN-JACQUES ROUSSEAU (1712–1778)

A. NATURAL EDUCATION

1. Rousseau presented his ideas on education in the novel *Emile*.
2. Rousseau argued that a "natural education" should replace the rigid schooling typical of his time. The key principles of a natural education included the following:
    ▸ *Children are naturally good and entitled to an education that emphasizes freedom and happiness.*
    ▸ *People develop through various stages, and individuals vary within these stages. Education must therefore be individualized since "every mind has its own form."*
    ▸ *Children should be encouraged to draw their own conclusions from experience. This principle anticipated what is now called "discovery learning."*

B. THE GENERAL WILL

1. *The Social Contract*, Rousseau's treatise on politics and government, is one of the most influential books on political theory in European history.
2. Thomas Hobbes and John Locke (see Chapter 8) argued that individuals entered a social contract with their rulers. In contrast, Rousseau argued that individuals entered into a social contract with one another. This created a community or organized civil society.
3. The sovereign power in a state does not lie in a ruler. Instead, it resides in the general will of the community as a whole. The

general will or "public spirit" is defined as any action that is right and good for all.

4. Rulers are servants of the community. If they fail to carry out the people's will, they should be removed.

5. Rousseau's concept of the general will and the sovereignty of the people influenced leaders of both the French and American revolutions. It is also important to note that twentieth-century dictators justified their rule by claiming to embody their nation's general will.

C. ROUSSEAU AND THE ENLIGHTENMENT

1. Like other philosophes, Rousseau was committed to defending individual freedom and changing the existing social order.

2. However, Rousseau distrusted reason and science. He trusted emotions and spontaneous feeling more than cold logic. As a result, Rousseau foreshadowed the romantic reaction to the Enlightenment.

Textbooks contain long lists devoted to discussing the contributions of leading philosophes. Voltaire and Rousseau generate by far the most questions. Be sure you know that Voltaire supported religious toleration and opposed superstition and ignorance. Test items on Rousseau stress his concept of the general will and his views of education as presented in the novel Emile.

X. THE NEW ECONOMICS

A. THE FRENCH PHYSIOCRATS

1. French economic reformers called physiocrats were the first to question mercantilist principles.

2. Led by Francois Quesnay, the physiocrats argued that economic activities should be freed from artificial restrictions. Governments should follow a laissez-faire policy of noninterference with the economy.

B. ADAM SMITH (1723–1790)

1. Adam Smith was the most influential advocate of laissez-faire economics.
2. Like Newton, Smith combined the thought of his predecessors into a single system based upon the study and application of natural laws.
3. Published in 1776, *The Wealth of Nations* is a landmark book that gave birth to classical economic thought.

C. KEY IDEAS IN *THE WEALTH OF NATIONS*

1. The role of government
   ▶ *Governments must not interfere with the free functioning of the market.*
   ▶ *Governments should limit their role to defending the state against foreign invasion, protecting property, and enforcing contracts.*
2. Free markets
   ▶ *In a free market, the economic laws of supply and demand will create a self-regulating economic system.*
   ▶ *Regulations such as tariffs hinder free trade and should be abolished.*
3. Self-interest and the "invisible hand"
   ▶ *Smith maintained that every individual is motivated by self-interest.*
   ▶ *Competition and self-interest are socially beneficial: "Self-interest drives people to action and the Invisible Hand of competition acts as an automatic regulator so that the market will generate wealth for a nation."*

D. <u>MAKING COMPARISONS</u>: THE ECONOMIC POLICIES OF JEAN-BAPTISTE COLBERT AND ADAM SMITH

1. Colbert
   ▶ *Believed that mercantilist policies offered the best way to increase French power and wealth*
   ▶ *Followed economic policies designed to give France a favorable balance of trade. Colbert promoted Caribbean sugar plantations, established slaving stations in Africa, and encouraged colonies in Canada*

▸ *Subsidized French industry by granting monopolies and enforcing high tariffs*

2. Adam Smith

    ▸ *Urged governments to abandon regulatory policies such as tariffs, trading monopolies, and navigation acts*

    ▸ *Advocated a policy of free trade and minimal government interference in the economy*

    ▸ *Believed that self-interested individuals working in a free market would increase production and wealth*

Peace, War, and Enlightened Despots, 1715–1789

I. CHARACTERISTICS OF THE EIGHTEENTH CENTURY

A. POLITICAL

1. Monarchy remained the most prevalent form of government.
2. Divine-right monarchy evolved into enlightened despotism in eastern Europe.
3. Aristocrats regained much influence. Powerful nobles and wealthy merchants influenced and sometimes dominated inept monarchs.

B. INTERNATIONAL RELATIONS

1. The great powers of Europe included Britain, France, Austria, Prussia, and Russia. Spain, Holland, Poland, Sweden, and the Ottoman Empire were no longer considered great powers.
2. The great powers fought limited wars:
   ‣ *Professional armies fought wars based on maneuver and strategy rather than bloody mass combat.*
   ‣ *Rulers fought wars for specific territorial and economic objectives.*
   ‣ *There were no religious wars among the great powers.*

C. THREE DISTINCTIVE PERIODS

1. A period of peace and prosperity from 1715 to 1740
2. A period of warfare from 1740 to 1763
3. A period of enlightened despotism from 1763 to 1789

II. PEACE AND PROSPERITY, 1715–1740

A. GROWING PROSPERITY

1. Great Britain emerged as Europe's leading commercial nation.
2. The upper classes benefited the most from the rising tide of commercial prosperity.
3. The labor of African slaves and eastern European serfs supported key commodities:
   ▸ *African slaves labored on immensely profitable Caribbean sugar plantations.*
   ▸ *Serfs labored in the rich grain-producing regions of eastern Europe.*

B. ENGLAND UNDER WALPOLE

1. The first two Hanoverian monarchs spoke little English and exercised little real power.
2. A ruling aristocracy of landed gentry and wealthy merchants dominated Parliament.
3. Robert Walpole emerged as England's first prime minister. Walpole led the Whig party in Parliament and was the government's leading minister.

C. FRANCE UNDER LOUIS XV

1. Louis XV (reigned 1715–1774) was a weak leader who was dominated by his royal mistresses and court favorites.
2. The nobles regained much of the power and privileges they lost during the reign of Louis XIV.
3. Although France was a prosperous and potentially powerful country, government debts continued to mount.

III. WARFARE, 1740–1763

A. GREAT POWER RIVALRIES

1. The Hohenzollerns of Prussia and the Habsburgs of Austria vied for power in central Europe.

2. The British and the French vied for trade in North America, the West Indies, and India.

B. THE WAR OF THE AUSTRIAN SUCCESSION, 1740–1748

1. The Austrian-Prussian rivalry
   - *The Pragmatic Sanction guaranteed Maria Theresa's (reigned 1740–1780) right to inherit the Habsburg throne and territories.*
   - *Frederick the Great ignored the Pragmatic Sanction and seized Silesia. Located on the northeastern frontier of Bohemia, Silesia boasted a million people, a prosperous linen industry, and rich deposits of iron ore.*
   - *Supported by France, Frederick's army successfully captured Silesia.*

2. The Anglo-French rivalry
   - *In Europe, the French supported Prussia and the English supported Austria.*
   - *In Canada, American colonists captured the French fortress of Louisbourg.*
   - *In India, the French seized Madras from the British.*

3. The Treaty of Aix-la-Chapelle
   - *Frederick retained control of Silesia, thus confirming Prussia's status as a great power and chief rival of Austria in German affairs.*
   - *The English restored Louisbourg to France, and the French gave Madras back to England.*

C. THE DIPLOMATIC REVOLUTION

1. The Austrian chancellor, Count Kaunitz, vowed to recover Silesia.
2. Kaunitz successfully formed a coalition that included France, Austria, and Russia. One consequence of this new alliance was the marriage of Marie Antoinette, daughter of Maria Theresa, to the future Louis XVI of France.
3. England then formed an alliance with Prussia to implement its policy of maintaining a balance of power on the continent.

CHRONOLOGICAL REVIEW

4. Note that this diplomatic revolution did not change the basic rivalries between England and France and Austria and Prussia.

D. THE SEVEN YEARS' WAR, 1756–1763

1. The colonial war
   - ▶ *In Canada, the British defeated the French and gained control of Quebec.*
   - ▶ *In the West Indies, the British gained control of major French sugar islands.*
   - ▶ *In India, the British gained control over key French trading posts.*
2. The war on the Continent
   - ▶ *The anti-Prussian alliance achieved a series of victories that threatened to crush Prussia.*
   - ▶ *Prussia was saved from defeat when Russia's new tsar, Peter III (reigned 1762), who admired Frederick the Great, dropped out of the war.*

E. THE TREATY OF PARIS, 1763

1. The British acquired French Canada and the land between the Appalachian Mountains and the Mississippi River.
2. France retained her Caribbean sugar islands and a few commercial installations in India.
3. Prussia retained possession of Silesia.

Test Tip

The great power rivalries and wars that took place between 1740 and 1763 can be confusing. It is important to remember that Prussia kept Silesia and that the British strengthened their global empire.

ENLIGHTENED DESPOTISM, 1763–1789

A. THE CONCEPT OF ENLIGHTENED DESPOTISM

1. The philosophes urged Europe's absolute rulers to use their power for the good of the people.

2. Enlightened despots would combat ignorance and superstition by eliminating irrational customs, promoting religious toleration, reforming legal codes, and supporting education.

3. It is important to note that the philosophes did not support democracy. Like Thomas Hobbes (see chapter 8), they believed that the people could not be trusted with self-government.

4. George III of England (reigned 1760–1820) and Louis XV of France (reigned 1715–1774) had little or no interest in either the philosophes or the concept of enlightened despotism. Catherine the Great of Russia, Frederick the Great of Prussia, and Joseph II of Austria were Europe's best-known enlightened despots.

B. CATHERINE THE GREAT (REIGNED 1762–1796)

1. Enlightened reforms
    ▸ *Corresponded with Voltaire and invited Denis Diderot to visit her court*
    ▸ *Supported Russia's first private printing presses*
    ▸ *Restricted the practice of torture*
    ▸ *Allowed limited religious toleration to Jews*
    ▸ *Convened a legislative commission to draft a new enlightened law code. However, the nobles refused to concede any of their privileges and very little was accomplished.*

2. Pugachev's Rebellion
    ▸ *From 1773 to 1775, a Cossack soldier named Emelian Pugachev led a dangerous uprising of serfs living along the Volga River. The rebellion finally ended when Pugachev was captured, tortured, and executed.*

▸ *Pugachev's Rebellion marked the end of Catherine's program of enlightened reforms.*

▸ *Determined to prevent any future rebellions, Catherine gave the nobles additional privileges and absolute power over their estates and serfs.*

3. Territorial expansion

▸ *Catherine ignored the philosophes' arguments against war. During her reign, Russia gained territory at the expense of the Ottoman Empire and Poland.*

▸ *Catherine's armies defeated the Ottomans and gained control over the Crimean Peninsula and most of the northern shore of the Black Sea.*

▸ *Catherine along with Prussia and Austria annexed Polish territory in a series of partitions that took place in 1772, 1793, and 1795. As a result of these partitions, Poland disappeared as an independent nation.*

C. FREDERICK THE GREAT (REIGNED 1740–1786)

1. Enlightened reforms

▸ *Called himself "the first servant of the state."*

▸ *Invited Voltaire to live in his palace at Potsdam*

▸ *Supported scientific agriculture*

▸ *Prepared a unified national code of law*

▸ *Abolished the use of torture except for treason and murder*

▸ *Encouraged Huguenots from France and Jews from Poland to immigrate to Prussia*

2. The Junkers and serfs

▸ *A firm believer in social order, Frederick strengthened the Junker's privileges.*

▸ *The Junkers retained full control over their serfs.*

D. <u>MAKING COMPARISONS:</u> PETER THE GREAT AND FREDERICK THE GREAT

1. Goals
   - ▶ *Both Peter the Great (see Chapter 10) and Frederick the Great were determined to transform their countries into great powers.*
   - ▶ *Both Peter the Great and Frederick the Great imported Western ideas to accelerate the pace of change.*

2. Policies
   - ▶ *Both rulers waged wars to conquer strategic territory.*
   - ▶ *Peter's victory over Sweden enabled Russia to take over warm-water outlets and become the leading Baltic power. Frederick's victory over Austria enabled Prussia to take control over Silesia and become a leading German power.*
   - ▶ *Both rulers imported Western ideas. Peter took the unprecedented step of visiting western Europe. His program of westernization opened Russia to new ideas, crops, and technologies. Frederick took the unprecedented step of inviting Voltaire to live in Prussia. His program of enlightened despotism opened Prussia to religious toleration, scientific agriculture, and a new code of laws.*
   - ▶ *Both rulers instituted changes that affected only the top layers of their societies. The serfs in both Russia and Prussia remained tied to the land and completely dominated by nobles.*

E. JOSEPH II (REIGNED 1780–1790)

1. Enlightened reforms
   - ▶ *Abolished serfdom and feudal dues*
   - ▶ *Abolished the system of forced labor known as the robot*
   - ▶ *Proclaimed religious toleration for all Christians and Jews*

> ▸ *Reduced the influence of the church*
> ▸ *Reformed the judicial system*
> ▸ *Abolished torture and ended the death penalty*

2. Protest and reaction

> ▸ *The nobles bitterly opposed Joseph's program of reforms.*
> ▸ *Following Joseph's death, the new emperor, Leopold II, placated the nobles by repealing many of Joseph's reforms.*
> ▸ *Serfdom and the robot remained in effect until 1848.*

Test Tip

The enlightened despots have generated a significant number of both multiple-choice and free-response questions on the APEURO exam. You should be able to discuss the extent to which Catherine the Great, Frederick the Great, and Joseph II succeeded and failed as enlightened despots.

Life and Culture in Eighteenth-Century Europe

I. THE AGRICULTURAL REVOLUTION

A. TRADITIONAL AGRICULTURAL PRODUCTION

1. In the early 1700s, peasants living in village communities farmed much of the land in western Europe.
2. Peasant farmers used an open-field system that included these characteristics:
    - *Animals grazed on the common or open lands.*
    - *Villagers divided the remaining land into long, narrow strips. Fences and hedges did not divide this open land.*
    - *Peasants traditionally used a two- or three-field system of crop rotation. This system was intended to restore exhausted soil. In practice, it meant that one-third to one-half of the land was allowed to lie fallow on any given year.*

B. INNOVATIONS IN THE LOW COUNTRIES

1. Reasons for Low Country leadership in farming
    - *The Low Countries were the most densely populated region in Europe. Dutch farmers were thus forced to seek maximum yields from their lands.*
    - *The Low Countries contained a growing urban population that created demand for farm products.*
2. New innovations in the Low Countries
    - *Enclosed fields*
    - *Continuous crop rotation*
    - *Use of manure as fertilizer*

▶ *Planting of a variety of crops*

▶ *Use of drainage to reclaim marshes*

C. ENGLISH AGRICULTURE

1. Agricultural innovators

    ▶ *Charles "Turnip" Townshend advocated continuous crop rotation using turnips, wheat, barley, and clover.*

    ▶ *Jethro Tull invented a seed drill that allowed for sowing crops in a straight row.*

    ▶ *Robert Bakewell pioneered selective breeding of livestock.*

2. The enclosure movement

    ▶ *English landowners consolidated previously scattered pasture lands into compact fields enclosed by fences and hedges.*

    ▶ *The new enclosed farmland enabled landowners to rapidly implement agricultural innovations. This encouraged the development of market-oriented agricultural production.*

    ▶ *The enclosure movement forced many poor rural people to move to cities and work in factories.*

The enclosure movement has generated a number of multiple-choice questions on the APEURO exam. It is important to remember that during most of the eighteenth century, the enclosure of common land primarily took place in the Low Countries and England. Peasants in France and Germany successfully resisted the enclosure of their open fields.

II. THE POPULATION EXPLOSION

A. FACTORS LIMITING POPULATION GROWTH

1. Periodic crop failures caused widespread famine.

2. Epidemic diseases such as bubonic plague decimated Europe's population.

3. Frequent wars destroyed crops and spread contagious diseases. For example, the Thirty Years' War reduced the population of the German states by at least one-third.

B. FACTORS PROMOTING POPULATION GROWTH

1. The agricultural revolution produced a more abundant food supply.
2. The potato became a key food staple during the eighteenth century. A single acre of potatoes could feed a family for a year.
3. Advances in transportation reduced the impact of local crop failures.
4. Eighteenth-century wars were fought by professional armies with specific geographic and economic objectives. As a result, eighteenth-century wars were less destructive than the seventeenth-century religious wars.
5. It is important to note that medical advances did not play an important role in eighteenth-century population growth.

C. POPULATION STATISTICS

1. Europe's population increased from 120 million in 1700 to 190 million in 1800.
2. The population of England rose from 6 million in 1750 to more than 10 million in 1800.
3. The population of France increased from 18 million in 1715 to 26 million in 1789.

III. LIFE IN THE EIGHTEENTH CENTURY

A. MARRIAGE AND THE FAMILY BEFORE 1750

1. Most young married European couples lived in nuclear families. Large multigenerational households were not the norm.
2. Most couples postponed marriage until they were in their mid- to late twenties.

3. Couples delayed marriage in order to acquire land or learn a trade.

4. A combination of parental authority and strict laws exercised tight control over marriage.

B. PATTERNS OF MARRIAGE AND THE FAMILY AFTER 1750

1. The growth of the cottage industry increased income and helped young people become financially independent.

2. As income rose, arranged marriages declined.

3. Increased mobility reduced parental and village controls.

4. Young peasant women increasingly left home to work as domestic servants.

C. CHILD REARING

1. Because of the high mortality rate among infants, parents were reluctant to become emotionally attached to their children.

2. Jean-Jacques Rousseau (see Chapter 11) encouraged parents to provide a warm and nurturing environment for their children.

3. Upper-middle-class parents began to place a greater emphasis on child rearing.

D. INCREASED LIFE EXPECTANCY

1. During the eighteenth century, the life spans of Europeans increased from 25 to 35 years.

2. New foods such as the potato combined with better farming techniques improved the diet of the poor.

3. Improved sanitation and the beginning of the science of immunology reduced death rates. Edward Jenner performed the first smallpox vaccination in 1796. The conquest of smallpox was the greatest medical triumph of the eighteenth century.

IV. THE RISE AND FALL OF WITCHCRAFT

A. WITCHCRAFT PERSECUTIONS

1. During the sixteenth and seventeenth centuries, between 100,000 and 200,000 people were officially tried for witchcraft.
2. Between 40,000 and 60,000 people were executed for witchcraft.
3. Elderly, widowed women were the most likely to be accused of witchcraft.

B. REASONS FOR THE GROWTH OF EUROPEAN WITCH HUNTS

1. Religious reformers stressed the great powers of the Devil. The Devil's diabolical activities reinforced the widespread belief in witchcraft.
2. Women were believed to be weak and thus susceptible to the Devil's temptations.
3. Religious wars and economic uncertainty caused great social and economic stress. Older, widowed women usually lacked power and thus became convenient scapegoats.

C. REASONS FOR THE DECLINE OF WITCHCRAFT

1. Religious wars finally came to an end, thus restoring social stability.
2. Protestants emphasized the concept of a supreme God, thus making the Devil seem less threatening.
3. The Scientific Revolution and the Enlightenment emphasized reason and uniform laws of nature. Support for superstition and witchcraft declined as educated Europeans turned to rational explanations of natural events.

APEURO test writers have devoted a number of multiple-choice and free-response questions to witchcraft. It is important to remember that witchcraft trials and executions most often affected elderly widows. Make sure that you study the reasons for both the growth and the decline of witchcraft.

CHRONOLOGICAL REVIEW

V. MAJOR ARTISTIC STYLES

A. ROCOCO

1. Basic characteristics
   - *The Rococo style reached its peak of popularity during the reign of Louis XV (1715–1774).*
   - *Artists depicted lighthearted and often frivolous scenes of "nobles at play."*
   - *Paintings featured light-colored pastels.*
   - *Architecture featured highly decorated interior ceilings.*
2. Leading artists and works
   - *Antoine Watteau,* Pilgrimage to Cythera
   - *François Boucher,* Cupid a Captive
   - *Jean-Honoré Fragonard,* The Swing

B. NEOCLASSICAL ART

1. Basic characteristics
   - *Neoclassical style supplanted Rococo during the 1780s.*
   - *Key figures were depicted as classical heroes.*
   - *Works portrayed the classical virtues of self-sacrifice and devotion to the state.*
   - *Compositions emphasized the Greek ideals of restraint, simplicity, and symmetry.*
2. Leading artists and works
   - *Jacques-Louis David,* Oath of the Horatii
   - *Jean-Antoine Houdon,* Voltaire Seated
   - *Thomas Jefferson,* Monticello

The French Revolution and Napoleon, 1789–1815

I. THE OLD REGIME

A. PEASANT DISTRESS

1. Peasants comprised over four-fifths of France's 26 million people.
2. Peasants lost half their income in taxes. They paid feudal dues to nobles, tithes to the church, and royal taxes to the king's agents. In addition, they paid a land tax called the taille and performed forced labor called the corvee.
3. Grain shortages led to sharp increases in the price of bread. The rising cost of bread was a major cause of discontent.

B. GOVERNMENT DEBT

1. Louis XIV's profligate spending left a massive public debt that consumed half the nation's tax revenues.
2. The cost of fighting the Seven Years' War and financing the American War for Independence worsened the fiscal crisis.

C. ARISTOCRATIC RESISTANCE

1. French nobles were exempt from paying taxes.
2. The nobles successfully resisted all attempts to reform the tax system.

D. ROYAL WEAKNESS

1. Louis XV (reigned 1715–1774) was a weak and indecisive ruler.

2. Louis XVI (reigned 1774–1792) and his Austrian wife Marie Antoinette were particularly unpopular and frivolous.

3. The high court of Paris—the Parlement—assumed the right to approve or disapprove the king's decrees, thus further eroding royal power.

II. THE ESTATES GENERAL

A. CALLING THE ESTATES GENERAL

1. By the spring of 1789, the French government faced the imminent threat of bankruptcy.

2. The refusal of the Assembly of Notables to support Louis XVI's program of tax reform forced the king to call a meeting of the Estates General.

B. THE THREE ESTATES

1. The first estate: the clergy
   ▸ *The Catholic Church held about 20 percent of the land.*
   ▸ *The French clergy paid no direct taxes. Instead, they gave the government a "free gift" of about 2 percent of their income.*

2. The second estate: the nobility
   ▸ *Nobles comprised 2 to 4 percent of the population.*
   ▸ *Nobles owned about 25 percent of the land.*

3. The third estate: everyone else
   ▸ *The third estate comprised 95 percent of the population.*
   ▸ *It included a diverse group of peasant farmers, urban workers, middle-class shopkeepers, wealthy merchants, and successful lawyers.*
   ▸ *Those in this group resented aristocratic privileges.*

C. THE TENNIS COURT OATH, JUNE 1789

1. Members of the first and second estates assumed that each estate would receive one vote. This system would enable them to impose their will on the third estate.

2. Led by Abbé Sieyès, the third estate rejected this method of voting and demanded that all three estates meet together.

3. When the king refused, the third estate declared itself the true National Assembly of France. Locked out of their official meeting place, the third estate met in a nearby indoor tennis court where they took an oath not to disband until they drafted a constitution.

4. The Tennis Court Oath marked the beginning of the French Revolution.

 ## THE NATIONAL ASSEMBLY, 1789–1791

A. THE STORMING OF THE BASTILLE

1. Determined to reassert royal authority, Louis XVI ordered a mercenary army of Swiss guards to march toward Paris and Versailles.

2. In Paris, angry mobs were already protesting the soaring price of bread. As tensions rose, a mob stormed the Bastille, a royal fortress and prison. The mob freed a handful of prisoners and seized the Bastille's supply of gunpowder and weapons.

3. The fall of the Bastille marked an important symbolic act against royal despotism. It also pushed Paris to the forefront of the ongoing revolution.

B. THE DECLARATION OF THE RIGHTS OF MAN AND THE CITIZEN, AUGUST 1789

1. The declaration proclaimed that all men were "born and remain free and equal in rights." These natural rights included the rights to "liberty, property, security, and resistance to oppression."

2. The declaration provided for freedom of religion, freedom from arbitrary arrest, freedom of speech and the press, and the right to petition the government.

CHRONOLOGICAL REVIEW

C. THE RIGHTS OF WOMEN

1. Women gained increased rights to inherit property and to divorce.

2. Women did not gain the right to vote or to hold political office.

3. In her book, *A Vindication of the Rights of Women*, Mary Wollstonecraft argued that women are not naturally inferior to men. The appearance of inferiority is created by a lack of education.

D. WOMEN'S MARCH TO VERSAILLES, OCTOBER 1789

1. On October 5, 1789, thousands of women marched to Versailles demanding cheap bread and insisting that the royal family move to Paris.

2. The king quickly capitulated, and a few days later the National Assembly also moved to Paris.

E. THE CIVIL CONSTITUTION OF THE CLERGY, AUGUST 1790

1. This act, passed by the National Assembly, did the following:
   ▸ *Confiscated the lands owned by the Roman Catholic Church*
   ▸ *Decreed that bishops and priests would be elected by the people and paid by the state*
   ▸ *Required the clergy to take a loyalty oath to support the new government*

2. It is important to note that Pope Pius VI condemned the act and that over half of the clergy refused to take the oath of allegiance. Alienated Catholics proved to be persistent opponents of the French Revolution.

F. REFORMS OF THE NATIONAL ASSEMBLY

1. The National Assembly did
   ▸ *create a constitutional monarchy*
   ▸ *divide France into 83 departments governed by elected officials*

▶ *establish the metric system of measurement*
▶ *abolish internal tariffs*
▶ *abolish guilds*

2. The National Assembly did *not*
   ▶ *abolish private property*
   ▶ *give women the right to vote*

IV. THE LEGISLATIVE ASSEMBLY, 1791–1792

A. FACTIONS IN THE LEGISLATIVE ASSEMBLY

1. Members of the Legislative Assembly sat together in separate sections of the meeting hall. The political terms *right*, *center*, and *left* are derived from this seating arrangement.
2. Conservatives who supported the king made up the Right.
3. Moderates comprised a large group in the Center.
4. Radicals who distrusted the king and wanted the Revolution to continue sat to the left. The Left was divided into two groups:
   ▶ *The Jacobins wanted to overthrow the monarchy and create a republic. Key Jacobin leaders included Jean-Paul Marat, Georges-Jacques Danton, and Maximilien Robespierre. It is important to note that the Marquis de Lafayette was not a Jacobin.*
   ▶ *The Girondists wanted to involve France in a war that would discredit the monarchy and extend France's revolutionary ideals across Europe.*

Test Tip

Make sure that you can identify both the Jacobins and the Girondists. It is important to remember that Lafayette was not a Jacobin. Also keep in mind that the Girondists favored using war to spread French revolutionary ideals.

CHRONOLOGICAL REVIEW

B. FRANCE VERSUS AUSTRIA AND PRUSSIA

1. Leopold II of Austria and Frederick William II of Prussia issued the Declaration of Pillnitz (August 1791) declaring that the restoration of absolutism in France was of "common interest to all sovereigns of Europe."
2. The Legislative Assembly declared war against Austria and Prussia in April 1792, thus beginning the War of the First Coalition.
3. The war began badly for the poorly equipped French armies. By the summer of 1792, Austrian and Prussian armies were advancing toward Paris.

C. THE SECOND FRENCH REVOLUTION

1. Faced with defeat, recruits rushed to Paris singing the *Marseillaise*, a stirring appeal to save France from tyranny. The rejuvenated French forces stopped the Austro-Prussian army, thus saving the Revolution.
2. During the summer of 1792, radicals called sans-culottes (literally "without breeches") took control of the Paris Commune (city government). The revolutionary Paris Commune intimidated the Legislative Assembly into deposing Louis XVI and issuing a call for the election of a national convention. This new body would then form a more democratic government.
3. Violence once again exploded in Paris. Convinced that royalists would betray the Revolution, mobs of sans-culottes executed over a thousand priests, bourgeoisie, and aristocrats. These "September massacres" marked the beginning of a second French Revolution dominated by radicals.

V. The National Convention, 1792–1795

A. THE EXECUTION OF LOUIS XVI

1. The newly elected National Convention abolished the monarchy and declared that France was now a republic.

2. The National Convention then had to decide Louis XVI's fate. The Girondists favored imprisonment while the Jacobins demanded that he be executed as a tyrant and a traitor.

3. After a contentious debate, the National Convention passed a resolution condemning Louis XVI to death. The resolution passed by one vote.

4. Supported by the sans-culottes, the Jacobins branded the Girondins as counterrevolutionaries and ousted them from the National Convention.

B. EUROPEAN REACTION

1. At first, European liberals supported the French Revolution and applauded the fall of the Old Regime.

2. The English statesman Edmund Burke offered a conservative critique of the French Revolution. Burke warned that mob rule would lead to anarchy and ultimately military dictatorship. To many moderate Europeans, the September massacres and the execution of Louis XVI vindicated Burke's dire predictions.

C. FOREIGN AND DOMESTIC THREATS

1. England, Spain, Holland, and Sardinia joined Prussia and Austria to form the First Coalition. In the spring of 1793, First Coalition armies converged on France.

2. Internal strife also threatened the National Convention. Girondists and royalist Catholics rebelled against the tyranny of radical Jacobins.

D. THE REIGN OF TERROR

1. Faced with foreign invaders and the threat of domestic rebellion, the National Convention established the Committee of Public Safety to defend France and safeguard the Revolution.

2. Led by Robespierre, the Committee of Public Safety exercised dictatorial power as it carried out a Reign of Terror.

3. In the name of creating a Republic of Virtue, Robespierre executed the queen, his chief rivals, and thousands of "dangerous" class enemies.

E. THE "NATION IN ARMS"

1. While the Terror crushed domestic dissent, Robespierre turned to the danger posed by the First Coalition. In 1793, the Committee of Public Safety proclaimed a "levée en masse" decreeing compulsory military service for all men between the ages of 18 and 40.

2. The levée en masse created a national military based upon mass participation. This marked the first example of the complete mobilization of a country for war.

3. Motivated by patriotism and led by a corps of talented young officers that included Napoleon Bonaparte, France's citizen-soldiers defeated the First Coalition's professional armies.

F. THE THERMIDORIAN REACTION

1. The Committee of Public Safety successfully crushed internal dissent and defeated the First Coalition. Despite these victories, Robespierre continued to pursue his fanatical dream of creating a Republic of Virtue.

2. Fearing for their lives and yearning for stability, the National Convention reasserted its authority by executing Robespierre.

3. Robespierre's death ended the radical phase of the French Revolution. On the new revolutionary calendar, July was called *Thermidor* from the French word for "heat." Hence, the revolt against Robespierre is called the Thermidorian reaction.

THE DIRECTORY, 1795–1799

A. BOURGEOISIE MISRULE

1. The government consisted of a two-house legislature and an executive body of five men known as the Directory.

2. Dominated by rich bourgeoisie, the Directory proved to be corrupt and unpopular.

B. THE FALL OF THE DIRECTORY

1. Public discontent mounted as the Directory failed to deal with inflation, food shortages, and corruption.

2. On November 9, 1799, an ambitious and talented young general named Napoleon Bonaparte overthrew the Directory and seized power.

VII. NAPOLEON AND THE CONSULATE, 1799–1804

A. THE FIRST CONSUL

1. Napoleon quickly took command of the new government. As first consul, he held all the power and made all the decisions.
2. Napoleon's popularity continued to rise as he restored order, stimulated prosperity, and defeated the Second Coalition.
3. Grateful voters overwhelmingly endorsed Napoleon's rule. He successfully used the democratic process to destroy democracy.
4. Secure in his power, Napoleon enacted policies designed to transform France into an efficient modern state.
5. It is interesting to note that in many ways Napoleon embodied the philosophes' concept of an enlightened despot.

B. THE NAPOLEONIC CODE

1. Napoleon's legal experts consolidated hundreds of local law codes into a uniform legal code that is still the basis of French law.
2. The new code guaranteed many achievements of the French Revolution, including equality before the law, freedom of religion, the abolition of privilege, and the protection of property rights.
3. The code increased the authority of husbands within the family. Women and children were legally dependent on their husband or father. For example, women could not buy or sell property without the consent of their husbands.

C. THE CONCORDAT OF 1801

1. Napoleon understood the importance of ending the strained relationship between the French government and the Catholic Church.

2. The Concordat of 1801 granted the Catholic Church special status as the religion of "the majority of Frenchmen." The pope regained the right to confirm church dignitaries appointed by the French government, depose French bishops, and reopen religious seminaries.

3. In return, the pope recognized the French government and accepted the loss of church properties confiscated during the Revolution.

D. THE LOSS OF LIBERTY

1. Napoleon censored the press and suppressed all political opposition.

2. Despite the loss of individual liberties, France enjoyed security, stability, and prosperity.

3. Supported by a grateful nation, Napoleon declared himself emperor on December 2, 1804.

VIII. THE NAPOLEONIC EMPIRE, 1804–1815

A. "EUROPE WAS AT MY FEET."

1. Between 1805 and 1807, Napoleon defeated Austria, Prussia, and Russia in a series of brilliant military victories.

2. Napoleon's victory at Austerlitz solidified his reputation as a military genius.

3. By 1808, French rule extended from the North Sea to Spain and included much of Italy.

4. It is important to note that Lord Nelson's naval victory at Trafalgar thwarted Napoleon's goal of controlling the seas and mounting an invasion of Great Britain.

B. THE REORGANIZATION OF GERMANY

1. Napoleon's victories enabled him to dissolve the Holy Roman Empire. He consolidated previously independent German states into a French-dominated Confederation of the Rhine.

2. Posing as a champion of the Revolution, Napoleon abolished feudalism and granted peasants freedom from manorial duties.
3. It is important to note that Napoleon unwittingly sparked a wave of German nationalism that fueled resistance to his rule. People who at first welcomed the French as liberators now felt they were being exploited by foreign invaders. Napoleon thus inadvertently accelerated the cause of German unification.

C. THE FALL OF NAPOLEON

1. Aura of invincibility
   - ▸ *Napoleon's appeared to be invincible. Many called him the greatest military commander in European history.*
   - ▸ *Napoleon's insatiable desire for power led him to make three disastrous mistakes that led to his downfall.*
2. The Continental System
   - ▸ *In 1806, Napoleon closed all European ports to British ships and goods.*
   - ▸ *Napoleon hoped that his Continental System would create a depression in Great Britain while promoting French prosperity.*
3. Guerrilla warfare in Spain
   - ▸ *In 1808, Napoleon deposed Spain's Bourbon rulers and installed his brother Joseph. This ill-advised action outraged the Spanish people.*
   - ▸ *Bands of Spanish fighters known as guerrillas repeatedly ambushed French troops and then fled into hiding. During the next five years, France lost almost 300,000 men. These losses contributed to Napoleon's ultimate defeat.*
4. The invasion of Russia
   - ▸ *The Continental System prevented Russia from exporting grain to Great Britain. When Tsar Alexander I (reigned 1801–1825) refused to stop this vital trade, Napoleon prepared to invade Russia.*

▶ *Napoleon's Grand Army reached Moscow. However, Alexander refused to surrender, thus forcing Napoleon to retreat. A combination of bitterly cold weather, disease, and merciless Russian attacks decimated Napoleon's army.*

D. NAPOLEON'S FINAL BATTLES

1. Napoleon's enemies quickly took advantage of his weakness. Great Britain, Russia, Prussia, and Austria formed a Grand Alliance that defeated Napoleon at the Battle of Nations in October 1813.

2. The allied armies entered Paris in March 1814. Napoleon abdicated his throne and was exiled to the island of Elba.

3. In March 1815, Napoleon escaped from Elba and formed a new army. Led by Great Britain and Prussia, the Grand Alliance defeated Napoleon at the Battle of Waterloo in June 1815.

4. Napoleon abdicated a second time and was shipped to St. Helena, a remote island in the South Atlantic. Once the master of Europe, Napoleon now lived in lonely exile writing his memoirs. He died in 1821.

Test Tip

Napoleon's battles have fascinated generations of military historians. It is important to remember that APEURO test writers are not military historians. You should know that the battle of Austerlitz solidified Napoleon's reputation as a military genius. Otherwise, focus your study time on the impact Napoleon's conquests had in spreading nationalism and in dissolving the Holy Roman Empire.

Restoration, Romanticism, and Revolution, 1815–1848

I. THE SEARCH FOR STABILITY

A. FORCES OF THE PAST

1. Traditional institutions of power
   - ▶ *Monarchy*
   - ▶ *Aristocracy*
   - ▶ *Church*
   - ▶ *Patriarchal family*
2. Conservatism
   - ▶ *Believed that national, historic, and religious traditions are the essential foundations of any society*
   - ▶ *Maintained that all change should be gradual*
   - ▶ *Appealed to those who were frightened by the social disorder, violence, and terror fomented by the French Revolution*

B. FORCES OF THE FUTURE

1. Industrialization
   - ▶ *Began in Great Britain in the late eighteenth century*
   - ▶ *Strengthened the size and significance of business leaders, merchants, and the middle class*
   - ▶ *Created a new class of urban workers*
2. Liberalism
   - ▶ *Believed in natural rights that governments must protect.*
   - ▶ *Supported civil liberties including freedom from arbitrary arrest and imprisonment and guarantees for freedom of speech, the press, assembly, and religion*

▸ *Admired the British system of constitutional monarchy*
▸ *Favored representative government*
▸ *Opposed full democracy*
▸ *Advocated economic individualism and opposed government intervention in the economy*
▸ *Expressed little concern for the plight of urban workers*

3. Nationalism

▸ *Believed that a nation consists of a group of people who share similar traditions, history, and language*
▸ *Argued that every nation should be sovereign and include all members of a nationality*
▸ *Insisted that a person's greatest loyalty should be to a nation-state*
▸ *Stirred powerful forces for change*

 ## II. RESTORING THE OLD ORDER: THE CONGRESS OF VIENNA

A. PRINCE KLEMENS VON METTERNICH (1773–1859)

1. Austrian foreign minister and host for the Congress of Vienna
2. Committed to the principles of conservatism
3. Viewed liberalism and nationalism as threats to European stability and the survival of the Austrian Empire

B. THE PRINCIPLE OF LEGITIMACY

1. Legitimacy meant restoring ruling families that had been deposed by the French Revolution and Napoleon.
2. As the younger brother of Louis XVI, Louis XVIII returned as the legitimate Bourbon ruler of France.
3. Bourbon rulers were also returned to their thrones in Spain and Naples.
4. The Congress restored the House of Orange in Holland and the House of Savoy in Sardinia-Piedmont.

C. THE BALANCE OF POWER

1. The leaders at Vienna wanted to weaken France so that it would no longer be able to wage wars of aggression and threaten the balance of power.

2. At the same time, the victorious powers did not want to impose a punitive treaty that would humiliate and antagonize France.

3. France was forced to return to its 1790 borders and to pay an indemnity of 700 million francs. However, France was allowed to keep most of its overseas possessions, its army, and an independent government.

4. To keep France from renewing its drive for power, the Congress encircled France with strengthened powers:

   ▶ *The Austrian Netherlands was united with the Dutch Republic to form a single kingdom of the Netherlands.*

   ▶ *A group of 39 German states were loosely joined into a newly created German Confederation, dominated by Austria.*

   ▶ *The Congress recognized Switzerland as an independent and neutral nation.*

   ▶ *The kingdom of Sardinia in Italy was strengthened by the addition of Piedmont and Savoy.*

D. TERRITORIAL SETTLEMENTS

1. Russia acquired more Polish territory.

2. Sweden retained Norway.

3. Prussia acquired two-fifths of Saxony and territory in the Rhineland along the border of France.

4. Austria acquired the northern Italian provinces of Lombardy and Venetia as compensation for its loss of Belgium.

5. Britain gained valuable territories for its overseas empire, including Malta, the Cape of Good Hope, Trinidad, and Tobago.

E. EVALUATION

1. The Congress of Vienna enacted a settlement that was acceptable to both the victors and to France.

CHRONOLOGICAL REVIEW

2. It created a balance of power that lasted until the unification of Germany in 1871.

3. It underestimated the forces of liberalism and nationalism unleashed by the French Revolution.

III. MAINTAINING THE OLD ORDER: THE CONCERT OF EUROPE

A. THE CONGRESS SYSTEM

1. England, Austria, Prussia, and Russia formed a Quadruple Alliance committing them to preserve the conservative order.

2. The great powers also agreed to hold periodic meetings or congresses to prevent crises from escalating into wider wars.

3. The effort to achieve consensus on foreign policy issues was known as the Concert of Europe. It marks the first significant experiment in collective security.

B. REVOLT AND REPRESSION

1. The Congress of Vienna disappointed liberals and nationalists across Europe. Discontentment led to revolts that tested Metternich and the Concert of Europe.

2. Uprisings in Spain and Italy

   ▸ *The repressive policies of the restored Spanish Bourbon King Ferdinand VII provoked demands for a more representative government. Acting with the consent of the other great powers, the French forces intervened, enabling Ferdinand to regain absolute power.*

   ▸ *Repressive monarchs in Naples and Sardinia-Piedmont also sparked rebellions. Metternich promptly responded by sending in Austrian forces who defeated the rebels.*

3. Repression in Germany

   ▸ *Young Germans continued to hope for liberal reforms and a united Germany. Disillusioned by the Congress of Vienna, they formed student associations to discuss their concerns.*

▸ *Alarmed by these student activists, Metternich persuaded the major German states to issue the Carlsbad Decrees. The decrees dissolved the student associations, censored books and newspapers, and used secret police to harass dissidents.*

4. The Decembrist Revolt in Russia

▸ *When Tsar Alexander I died in December 1825, a group of army officers rebelled, calling for constitutional reform.*

▸ *Alexander's successor, Nicholas I (reigned 1825–1855) ruthlessly suppressed the Decembrists.*

▸ *Under Nicholas I's oppressive regime, Russia became Europe's most powerful reactionary stronghold.*

 IV. ROMANTICISM

A. THE ROMANTIC MOVEMENT

1. Swept across Europe during the first half of the nineteenth century
2. Influenced religion, art, music, and philosophy
3. Inspired a desire for freedom of thought, feeling, and action

B. KEY CHARACTERISTICS

1. The primacy of emotion

▸ *The Enlightenment stressed reason as a way to understand nature.*

▸ *Romantics rejected reason, and instead stressed emotion, intuition, and subjective feelings.*

2. A different past

▸ *Neoclassical artists looked to Greece and Rome for models of order and clarity.*

▸ *Romantics looked to the medieval period for models of chivalrous heroes, miraculous events, and unsolved mysteries.*

3. A new view of nature
  ▸ *Enlightened thinkers relied on the scientific method to study and understand nature. They viewed nature as a well-ordered machine.*
  ▸ *Romantics preferred to contemplate the beauty of nature. They were inspired by raging rivers, great storms, and majestic mountains veiled in mist.*

C. <u>MAKING COMPARISONS</u>: ENLIGHTENED AND ROMANTIC VIEWS OF RELIGION

1. The Enlightenment embraced a mechanical view of human nature and the physical world. Enlightened thinkers rejected faith and instead relied on a rational, scientific approach to understand the relationship between human beings and the natural world. The Enlightenment favored the deist view that a distant God created the natural world and like a "divine watchmaker" stepped back from his creation and humanity's daily concerns.

2. The romantics believed in a loving, personal God. They stressed emotions, inner faith, and religious inspiration. Romantics embraced the wonders and mysteries of nature as a way to feel the divine presence.

D. KEY ROMANTIC WRITERS, ARTISTS, AND COMPOSERS

1. Writers
  ▸ *William Wordsworth and Samuel Taylor Coleridge, lyrical ballads*
  ▸ *Friedrich von Schiller,* Ode to Joy
  ▸ *Johann Wolfgang von Goethe,* Faust
  ▸ *Sir Walter Scott,* Ivanhoe
  ▸ *Victor Hugo,* The Hunchback of Notre Dame
  ▸ *Jacob and Wilhelm Grimm,* Grimm's Fairy Tales
2. Artists
  ▸ *Caspar David Friedrich,* Wanderer Above the Mist
  ▸ *Eugene Delacroix,* Liberty Leading the People
  ▸ *John Constable,* The Hay Wain

▸ *J. M. W. Turner,* Hannibal Crossing the Alps

▸ *Francisco Goya,* The Third of May 1808

3. Composers

    ▸ *Ludwig van Beethoven,* Ninth Symphony

    ▸ *Richard Wagner,* The Ring of the Nibelung

E. ROMANTICISM AND NATIONALISM

1. As romantic writers studied the past, they helped make people aware of their common heritage. The resurgence of national feeling sparked nationalist movements across Europe. The first stirring was felt in Greece.

2. Greek Independence

    ▸ *The Greek revolt against the Ottoman Empire began in 1821.*

    ▸ *While the revolutions in Spain and Italy failed because of great power intervention, the Greek revolt succeeded because of the support of Great Britain, France, and Russia. These nations all wanted to expand their influence in the Balkans. They were also influenced by public support for Greece because of its historic importance as the birthplace of Western civilization.*

The romantic movement is one of the most frequently tested APEURO topics. Multiple-choice questions focus on the romantic emphasis on emotion. Free-response questions focus on comparison between the Enlightenment and romantic views of nature.

V. LIBERAL REFORM IN ENGLAND

A. THE REFORM BILL OF 1832

1. The House of Commons was less representative of the British people than at any time in its 500-year history.

2. Many boroughs (electoral districts) were sparsely populated, and a few had no people at all. Meanwhile, new industrial cities such as Manchester had no representatives.

3. After a decade of pressure from factory owners and merchants, Parliament passed the Reform Bill of 1832. It created a number of new districts representing heavily urban areas. It also doubled the number of voters to include most middle-class men.

4. It is important to note that under the Reform Bill of 1832 only about one in five adult males could vote. Workers, women, and the poor were all disenfranchised.

B. THE REPEAL OF THE CORN LAWS

1. The Corn Laws placed a high tariff on imported corn, wheat, and other grains. The tariff benefitted large landowners by providing them with a protected market for their crops.

2. Prominent industrialists formed the Anti-Corn Law League. They advocated a free-trade policy that would lower the price of food and increase the profits of industry.

3. Wealthy landowners stubbornly resisted all reform proposals. However, the Irish potato famine dramatically strengthened support for cheaper imported grains.

4. Parliament finally voted to repeal the Corn Laws in 1846. This marked a victory for Britain's urban population and for the proponents of free trade.

C. THE CHARIST MOVEMENT

1. Britain's disenfranchised workers demanded more sweeping reforms.

2. In 1838, working-class leaders drew up a People's Charter that demanded universal manhood suffrage, a secret ballot, equal electoral districts, and the abolition of property requirements for membership in the House of Commons.

3. Despite widespread public support, Parliament adamantly refused to consider the Chartists' proposals. It is important to note that most of the Chartist reforms would be ultimately adopted.

THE REVOLUTIONS OF 1830

A. THE FRENCH REVOLUTION OF 1830

1. In 1824, Charles X (reigned 1824–1830) succeeded his brother, Louis XVIII. A dedicated reactionary, Charles X vigorously opposed republicanism, liberalism, and constitutionalism.
2. Charles X's reactionary policies infuriated both his liberal and working-class opponents.
3. Discontent with Charles X's arbitrary policies ignited three days of rioting in July 1830. Eugene Delacroix captured the spirit of the uprising in his famous painting, *Liberty Leading the People*.
4. Delacroix's tribute to liberty portrayed a unified people dedicated to overthrowing tyranny. The unity proved to be brief. While the workers wanted a republic, the bourgeoisie wanted a constitutional monarchy.
5. The bourgeoisie prevailed. With their support, Louis Philippe, Duke of Orleans, became "king of the French." Louis Philippe prided himself on being a "citizen king" who supported France's business interests.

B. REVOLUTION IN BELGIUM

1. The July Revolution in France helped spark discontent in Belgium.
2. The Congress of Vienna united the Austrian Netherlands (Belgium) with Holland to form a single kingdom of the Netherlands.
3. Catholic Belgium and Protestant Holland had very little in common. In 1830, riots in Belgium quickly turned into a widespread demand for independence.
4. Both Great Britain and France opposed intervention. In 1830, the great powers recognized Belgium as a neutral state.

C. ITALIAN NATIONALISM

1. Austria dominated northern Italy.

2. Italian nationalists formed a secret society called the Carbonari ("charcoal burners"). The Carbonari hoped to drive out the Austrians and unify Italy.

3. Inspired by the events in France and Belgium, the Carbonari rebelled. However, Metternich promptly sent in Austrian troops to restore order.

4. The Carbonari's failure left Giuseppe Mazzini as Italy's foremost nationalist leader.

THE REVOLUTIONS OF 1848

A. CAUSES

1. Conservative leaders steadfastly refused to respond to the problems and social tensions created by industrialization and urbanization.

2. Working-class radicals and middle-class liberals were convinced that the repressive Metternich system had outlived its usefulness.

3. Nationalists in Italy and Germany yearned for unification. At the same time, national minorities in the Austrian Empire demanded independence.

4. Widespread crop failures, rising prices of food, and growing unemployment helped fuel demands for change.

B. REVOLUTION IN FRANCE

1. Affluent bourgeoisie dominated France during the reign of Louis Philippe (reigned 1830–1848). A leading minister rejected demands for extending the franchise to the working class by proclaiming, "Enrich yourself and you will have the vote."

2. Unable to withstand public pressure, Louis Philippe's government collapsed in February 1848.

3. As tension and unrest gripped Paris, liberals, socialists, and Bonapartists all vied for power.

4. Following a bloody confrontation between workers and the capitalist-backed government, French voters overwhelmingly

elected Louis Napoleon as president of the Second French Republic. The nephew of Napoleon Bonaparte, Louis promised to restore order at home and glory abroad.

C. DEFEAT IN ITALY

1. Led by Giuseppe Mazzini, the "Young Italy" movement sought to establish a liberal republic embracing all Italy.
2. The Austrians once again proved to be too strong while the Italians once again proved to be too divided.

D. HOPE AND FAILURE IN ITALY

1. A growing number of German nationalists hoped for a more liberal German state.
2. In 1834, all the major German states except Austria formed the Zollverein, a free-trading union, to facilitate commerce.
3. Riots broke out in Berlin in 1848. Frederick William IV (reigned 1840–1861) responded by issuing a series of reforms, including calling a Prussian assembly to draft a new constitution.
4. Meanwhile, another assembly met in Frankfurt to draft a constitution for all Germany.
5. The hopes of German reformers were soon crushed. Supported by the army, Frederick William dissolved the Prussian assembly. He then rejected the Frankfurt assembly's plan for a constitutional monarchy declaring that he would refuse to "pick up a crown from the gutter."
6. The failure of the German reform movement had fateful consequences for Germany and the future of Europe.

E. REVOLUTIONS IN THE AUSTRIAN EMPIRE

1. Austria was a huge dynastic state in which a dominant German-speaking nation ruled a large number of subject nationalities and ethnic groups.
2. Revolutionary fervor quickly spread from Paris to Vienna. As tensions mounted, Metternich resigned and fled to England.
3. An Austrian constituent assembly abolished the robot, or forced labor, thus removing a major source of peasant discontent.

4. Revolution quickly spread from Vienna to Hungary where Louis Kossuth demanded self-government.

5. Despite initial setbacks, the Austrian government regained control. Only Hungary remained defiant. The new Austrian emperor Francis Joseph (reigned 1848–1916) accepted the offer of Tsar Nicholas I to help defeat the Hungarians. A joint invasion of Russian and Austrian forces crushed Hungarian resistance.

F. KEY POINTS

1. The revolutions of 1848 failed because of internal divisions, a lack of popular support outside the cities, and the continued strength of conservative forces.

2. Peaceful reforms enabled England to avoid violent revolts.

3. Repressive policies stifled reform in Russia.

4. The idealistic romantic spirit now yielded to a new age of political realism.

Test Tip

The revolutions of 1848 form a particularly complex sequence of events. Do not spend time memorizing the chronology of what happened. Instead, focus on the causes and consequences of the various revolutions.

The Industrial Revolution

I. REASONS FOR BRITISH LEADERSHIP

A. THE ENCLOSURE MOVEMENT

1. This movement, which privatized land formerly available to all for grazing and farming, concentrated land ownership in fewer hands.
2. With no land to work, small farmers were displaced, thus forming a pool of cheap labor.

B. THE AGRICULTURAL REVOLUTION

1. Crop rotation replaced the open-field system.
2. Landowners experimented with new crops such as turnips and new inventions such as the seed drill.

C. THE POPULATION EXPLOSION

1. New farming methods produced more food.
2. Medical advances such as Edward Jenner's discovery of a smallpox vaccine reduced death rates.
3. The combined population of Great Britain and Ireland increased from 10 million in 1750 to 30 million in 1850.

D. THE COMMERCIAL REVOLUTION

1. Successful British merchants had capital for investment.
2. Great Britain had the most highly developed banking system in Europe.

E. THE ENLIGHTENMENT

1. The Royal Society exchanged scientific ideas.
2. British society encouraged and rewarded inventors and entrepreneurs.

II. THE TEXTILE INDUSTRY

A. THE INCENTIVE

1. The global demand for cotton cloth was enormous.
2. Prompted by huge potential profits, British entrepreneurs financed new ways of spinning and weaving cotton.

B. THE INVENTIONS

1. In 1733, John Kay invented the flying shuttle, enabling a single weaver to work twice as fast.
2. In the mid-1760s, James Hargreaves invented the spinning jenny, a spinning machine that made it possible for a single weaver to work six to eight threads at a time.
3. In 1769, Richard Arkwright invented a water frame that used waterpower from fast-moving streams to drive spinning machines.
4. In 1779, Samuel Crompton invented a spinning machine called the mule that combined the best features of the spinning jenny and the water frame to produce thread that was stronger, finer, and more uniform than earlier spinning machines.
5. In 1785, Edmund Cartwright invented a power loom that used waterpower to dramatically speed up weaving.
6. In 1793, Eli Whitney invented the cotton gin, making it possible to efficiently remove seeds from the cotton fiber.
7. As a result of these continuous technological improvements, the output of cotton fiber from British textile factories rose from 40 million yards in 1785 to more than 2 billion yards in 1850.

APEURO test writers do not focus on the sequence of inventions that revolutionized the textile industry. Instead, you should know that these inventions marked a shift from human and animal power to mechanical power. The mechanization of the spinning and weaving process in the textile industry ushered in the Industrial Revolution.

C. THE STEAM ENGINE

1. James Watt patented the first steam engine in 1769.
2. The steam engine rapidly replaced waterpower in British textile factories.
3. Steam power played a key role in boosting iron production.

D. THE RAILROAD

1. Steam power enabled inventors to build railroad locomotives.
2. English entrepreneurs wanted a railroad line to connect the port of Liverpool with the inland city of Manchester, the heart of the spinning and weaving industry. The Liverpool-Manchester Railway opened in 1830.
3. By 1850, Britain had over 6,000 miles of railroad track.
4. Railroads had the following far-reaching effects:
    ▶ *Stimulated further industrial growth*
    ▶ *Created regional and national markets for agricultural and industrial goods*
    ▶ *Reduced the cost of shipping freight*
    ▶ *Promoted leisure travel*

III. GREAT BRITAIN'S INDUSTRIAL DOMINANCE

A. STATISTICAL MEASURES OF BRITISH PROSPERITY, 1850

1. Manufactured one-half of the world's cotton
2. Mined two-thirds of the world's coal
3. Mined more than one-half of the world's iron
4. Controlled one-third of the world's international trade

B. THE GREAT EXHIBITION, 1851

1. The exhibition was held to celebrate Britain's undisputed economic and technological dominance.
2. Britain's Hall of Machinery featured the locomotive engines, hydraulic presses, and power looms that had powered the Industrial Revolution.

C. <u>MAKING COMPARISONS:</u> THE CRYSTAL PALACE AND THE ARC DE TRIOMPHE

1. The Crystal Palace in London
   - *Commissioned to celebrate British leadership in the industrial age*
   - *Enclosed 18 acres and almost 1 million square feet of exhibition space*
   - *Featured prefabricated glass panels and cast-iron columns*
   - *Demonstrated the possibilities of mass production*
2. The Arc de Triomphe in Paris
   - *Commissioned to celebrate French victories during the Revolution and the Age of Napoleon*
   - *Based on the triumphal arches of ancient Rome*
   - *Combined a Neoclassical arch with romantic relief sculptures*
   - *Reached a height of 164 feet, making it the largest arch ever built*

IV. SOCIAL EFFECTS OF INDUSTRIALIZATION

A. THE FACTORY SYSTEM

1. The factory was a place where large numbers of workers used machines to manufacture goods.
2. As the factory system spread, the putting-out system disappeared.

B. WORKING-CLASS MISERY

1. Early factories exposed workers to dangerous machines and deadly diseases.
2. The demand for cheap labor led to the widespread employment of women and young children.
3. Workers had no health insurance and little job security.

C. URBANIZATION

1. The factory system transformed many small towns into crowded cities. For example, between 1760 and 1850, the population of Manchester surged from 15,000 to 300,000.
2. Between 1800 and 1850, the number of European cities with more than 100,000 inhabitants rose from 22 to 47.
3. Workers lived in crowded slums that lacked sanitation. Entire families lived in a single dark room.

D. MIDDLE-CLASS PROSPERITY

1. The middle classes, or bourgeoisie, enjoyed unprecedented prosperity, political power, and leisure time.
2. The *haute bourgeoisie* included wealthy bankers, merchants, and industrialists.
3. The *petite bourgeoisie* included shopkeepers, skilled artisans, professional men, and the clergy.

 # V. CLASSICAL BRITISH ECONOMIC THEORY

A. SHARED BELIEFS

1. Accepted the laissez-faire policies advocated in Adam Smith's *Wealth of Nations*.
2. Insisted that supply and demand would act as an "invisible hand" so that selfish individual acts would ultimately benefit the whole society.
3. Opposed government regulations that interfered with the competitive free market.

4. Believed government policies should be limited to enforcing contracts, protecting private property, and ensuring national defense.

B. THOMAS MALTHUS ON POPULATION

1. Malthus argued that human population grows geometrically, while food supply expands arithmetically.
2. He insisted that human population would inevitably outstrip food production, thus making famine and misery inevitable.

C. DAVID RICARDO ON WAGES

1. Influenced by Malthus's pessimistic appraisal of the plight of the working class, David Ricardo formulated the "iron law of wages."
2. According to Ricardo, labor is a commodity whose price is determined by the law of supply and demand.
3. Ricardo contended that increasing working-class wages would prompt laborers to have more children. As the supply of workers increased, their wages would decline.
4. The iron law of wages left no room for a better future for working-class families. It provided strong support for opposing labor unions and refusing to raise wages.

VI. WORKING-CLASS PROTEST IN GREAT BRITAIN

A. THE LUDDITES

1. Named after Ned Ludd, frustrated English workers known as Luddites broke into early textile factories and smashed the machinery.
2. These acts of despair could not stop the Industrial Revolution. Parliament quickly responded by passing a law making the destruction of machines a capital offense.
3. Workers gradually came to realize that destroying machines would not improve their lives. Instead, they had to form labor unions to fight for higher wages and better working conditions.

B. EARLY LABOR UNIONS

1. The Combination Acts of 1799 and 1800 prohibited British workers from organizing to improve their condition.
2. Under pressure from labor and middle-class reformers, Parliament repealed the Combination Acts in 1825.
3. In 1875, British trade unions won full legal status, including the right to strike.

VII. SOCIALISM

A. SHARED BELIEFS

1. The existing distribution of wealth is unjust. The "haves" possess more than they need while the "have-nots" possess barely enough to survive.
2. The resources and means of production should be owned by the community.
3. The profits of human labor should be equitably distributed.

B. UTOPIAN SOCIALISM

1. Charles Fourier, Louis Blanc, and Robert Owen were the most prominent Utopian Socialists.
2. They advocated social and economic planning to create societies based on cooperation rather than competition.
3. Although the Utopians founded a number of cooperative communities, their experiments all failed.

C. MARXIAN SOCIALISM

1. In the *Communist Manifesto*, Karl Marx and Friedrich Engels asserted that "the history of all hitherto existing societies is the history of class struggles."
2. Marx believed that the history of class conflict is best understood through the dialectical process of thesis, antithesis, and synthesis. The thesis is the dominant state of affairs. It inevitably gives rise to a conflicting or contradictory force called the antithesis. The resulting clash between the

thesis and the antithesis produces a new state of affairs called the synthesis.

3. Marx argued that nineteenth-century society had split "into two great classes directly facing each other: bourgeoisie and proletariat." As the owners of the means of production, the bourgeoisie were the thesis. The proletariat or workers were the antithesis.

4. Marx contended that a class struggle between the bourgeoisie and the proletariat would lead "to the dictatorship of the proletariat."

5. The "dictatorship of the proletariat" would be a transitional phase leading "to the abolition of all classes and to a classless society" in which there would be no private ownership of the means of production.

6. Marx and Engels argued that women were exploited by both men and capitalists.

Test Tip

Marxism is one of the most frequently tested topics on the APEURO exam. Test writers expect you to recognize famous quotes by Marx and Engels and identify key concepts such as the dialectical process, class conflict, the dictatorship of the proletariat, and classless society.

D. EDWARD BERNSTEIN AND EVOLUTIONARY SOCIALISM

1. Marx predicted that as the workers became more exploited they would unite to overthrow the bourgeoisie. Instead, as capitalism matured, working conditions improved.

2. Led by Edward Bernstein, "evolutionary" socialists began to revise Marxian doctrine to adjust to the new economic realities.

3. Bernstein rejected Marx's concept of class struggle and instead sought to achieve socialist goals by a process of gradual reform.

Nationalism, Realpolitick, and Realism: 1850–1871

I. NAPOLEON III (reigned 1852–1870)

A. ESTABLISHMENT OF THE SECOND EMPIRE

1. In 1848, French voters elected Louis Napoleon Bonaparte (nephew of Napoleon I) the new president of the Second French Republic.
2. Just four years later, Louis Napoleon proclaimed France an empire with himself Emperor Napoleon III. A vast majority of the French people endorsed these proclamations.

B. ECONOMIC PROGRESS

1. Napoleon III understood the importance of modern industrialization. His economic policies included the following achievements:
   ▶ *Railroad mileage increased by more than fivefold.*
   ▶ *Moderate free-trade policies doubled exports.*
   ▶ *Industrial production doubled, enriching the middle class.*
2. Napoleon did not ignore the working class. He legalized trade unions and improved public housing.

C. REBUILDING PARIS

1. Napoleon named Baron Georges Haussmann to oversee a vast project to redesign Paris.
2. Haussmann replaced narrow streets and congested working-class neighborhoods with wide avenues, impressive public monuments, and expansive parks.

3. The rebuilding project accomplished several objectives:
   ▸ *It transformed Paris into a symbol of France's prosperity and greatness.*
   ▸ *It made it much harder for rioters to blockade streets.*

D. QUEST FOR GLORY

1. Napoleon believed that the Concert of Europe (see Chapter 15) limited France's foreign policy.
2. Napoleon was determined to follow a foreign policy calculated to undermine the Concert of Europe and win international glory for himself and for France.

II. THE CRIMEAN WAR, 1853–1856

A. THE CAUSES

1. A squabble over jurisdiction within the holy places in Turkish-ruled Jerusalem brought France (the protector of the Catholics) and Russia (the protector of the Orthodox clergy) into diplomatic controversy with Turkey in the middle.
2. Tsar Nicholas I saw an opportunity to dominate Turkey and secure entrance into the Mediterranean through the Turkish Straits.
3. Austria felt threatened by Russia's expansion into the Balkans.
4. France and Britain opposed any change in the regional balance of power.

B. THE WAR

1. France, Britain, Turkey, and a contingent of 10,000 men from Piedmont-Sardinia captured the strongly defended Russian fortress at Sevanstopol.
2. The new Russian tsar, Alexander II, sued for peace after the fall of Sevanstopol.
3. The war claimed over 500,000 lives, most caused by disease and inadequate medical care.

C. CONSEQUENCES

1. The Crimean War marked the first great power conflict since the Congress of Vienna in 1815 (see Chapter 15).
2. Napoleon III achieved his objective of breaking the alliance between Austria and Russia.
3. By entering the war on the side of France and Britain, Piedmont-Sardinia hoped to gain support for Italian unification.
4. Russia's humiliating defeat forced Alexander II to launch an ambitious program of reforms.

III. RUSSIA: REACTION AND REFORM

A. TSARIST RUSSIA IN THE 1850s

1. Tsar Alexander II was an autocrat whose will was law.
2. Russia's aristocracy continued to own almost all the land and be exempt from taxes.
3. Russia had a very small middle class. Ninety-five percent of the people were peasants, most of whom were serfs.

B. ALEXANDER'S REFORMS

1. The emancipation of the serfs, 1861
   ▸ *In 1861, Alexander II issued an Emancipation Edict freeing the serfs.*
   ▸ *Although they were free, the peasants still did not own the land.*
2. The creation of zemstvos
   ▸ *In 1864, Alexander introduced a system of local and regional self-government through elected assemblies called zemstvos.*
   ▸ *Although the zemstvos did provide some opportunity for public discussion, they did not lead to the creation of a national assembly.*

IV. THE UNIFICATION OF ITALY

A. THE SITUATION IN 1850

1. Repeated failures
   - ▶ *The Carbonari had failed to incite a successful revolution.*
   - ▶ *Giuseppe Mazzini and the Young Italy Movement failed to rally support for a republic.*
2. Continued obstacles
   - ▶ *Austria continued to control Lombardy and Venetia while also dominating other small Italian states.*
   - ▶ *A reactionary Bourbon regime continued to control the kingdom of the Two Sicilies.*
   - ▶ *Pope Pius IX opposed the cause of Italian nationalism*
3. Piedmont leadership
   - ▶ *Italian nationalists looked to the kingdom of Piedmont-Sardinia for leadership. It was the only Italian state ruled by an Italian dynasty.*
   - ▶ *In 1852, Piedmont's King Victor Emmanuel II named Count Camillo di Cavour his prime minister.*

B. CAVOUR AND THE PRACTICE OF REALPOLITIK

1. Realpolitik
   - ▶ *Early Italian nationalists such as Mazzini had been inspired by romantic ideals of nationalism.*
   - ▶ *Cavour was a realist guided by the dictates of political power. He believed that shrewd diplomacy and well-chosen alliances were more useful than grand proclamations and romantic rebellions.*
   - ▶ *Cavour's successful combination of power politics and secret diplomacy is called Realpolitik, "the politics of reality."*
2. Strengthening Piedmont
   - ▶ *Cavour launched an ambitious economic program that included building railroads and expanding commerce.*
   - ▶ *Cavour modernized Piedmont's army.*

3. The Franco-Piedmont alliance

    ▸ *Cavour understood that Austria was the greatest obstacle to Italian unity.*

    ▸ *Cavour formed an alliance with Napoleon III to drive Austria out of northern Italy.*

C. WAR WITH AUSTRIA, 1859

1. The combined French and Piedmont armies defeated the Austrians. Meanwhile, Italian nationalists staged revolts across northern Italy.
2. Sardinia annexed all of northern Italy except Venetia.

D. GIUSEPPE GARIBALDI AND THE RED SHIRTS

1. The pragmatic Cavour and the romantic Garibaldi agreed that Italy should be freed from foreign control.
2. While Cavour was uniting the north, he also secretly supported Garibaldi in the south.
3. In May 1860, Garibaldi and his small but zealous force of so-called Red Shirts successfully invaded and liberated the kingdom of the Two Sicilies.
4. Garibaldi agreed to step aside and let Victor Emmanuel rule the areas he had conquered.

E. PERSISTENT PROBLEMS

1. In March 1861, an Italian parliament formally proclaimed the kingdom of Italy with Victor Emmanuel II as king "by the grace of God and the will of the nation." Tragically, Cavour died just two months later.
2. The newly unified kingdom of Italy faced a number of persistent problems:

    ▸ *Unification was still not complete. Venetia remained under Austrian control and the papacy led by Pius IX remained hostile to the new Italian state.*

CHRONOLOGICAL REVIEW

> ▶ Northern Italy was urban, sophisticated, and increasingly industrialized. Southern Italy remained rural, backward, and poor.
>
> ▶ The new government was burdened by a heavy debt.

Cavour and Garibaldi are compelling historic figures who command interest and APEURO questions. However, don't forget to study the often overlooked but still important problems that plagued the newly founded kingdom of Italy.

V. THE UNIFICATION OF GERMANY

A. THE SITUATION IN 1860

1. Obstacles to unity
   - ▶ Germany remained politically divided into a number of small states that jealously guarded their independence.
   - ▶ The German Confederation remained a loose grouping of 39 states dominated by Austria.
   - ▶ French foreign policy continued to support German rivalries while opposing Germany unity.

2. Prussia's growing strength
   - ▶ Prussia's population increased from 11 million in 1815 to more than 18 million in 1850.
   - ▶ Led by Prussia, the Zollverein (see Chapter 15) promoted German economic growth while demonstrating the advantages of unity.

B. OTTO VON BISMARCK, MASTER OF REALPOLITIK

1. In 1862, William I chose as his prime minister a Junker and staunch conservative named Otto von Bismarck.

2. A master of Realpolitik, Bismarck set out to strengthen Prussia.

3. Bismarck enlarged and reequipped the Prussian army so that he could take advantage of opportunities for further territorial expansion.

4. Disavowing liberalism as frivolous and misguided, Bismarck firmly declared, "The great questions of our day cannot be solved by speeches and majority votes—that was the great error of 1848 and 1849—but by blood and iron."

C. WAR WITH DENMARK, 1864

1. Bismarck led Prussia into war with Denmark to win two border provinces, Schleswig and Holstein.

2. The victory combined with shrewd diplomacy enabled Bismarck to begin the process of eliminating Austria from German affairs.

It has been said that only three people truly understood the controversy over Schleswig and Holstein. APEURO test writers do not expect you to be the fourth person to master this topic. As you study Bismarck and the wars with Denmark, Austria, and France, avoid getting bogged down in the details. Instead, focus on the consequences of each war.

D. WAR WITH AUSTRIA, 1866

1. The Seven Weeks' War
   - ▶ *In 1866, Bismarck provoked Austria into declaring war on Prussia.*
   - ▶ *Prussia's revitalized army easily crushed the Austrians in a brief conflict known as the Seven Weeks' War.*

2. Consequences
   - ▶ *Austria agreed to the dissolution of the German Confederation.*
   - ▶ *With Austria excluded from German affairs, Bismarck organized a North German Confederation dominated by Prussia.*
   - ▶ *As Prussia's ally, Italy annexed Venetia.*

E. WAR WITH FRANCE, 1870

1. The causes
    - ▶ *France feared the sudden emergence of a strong and aggressive Prussia. It is important to note that France had opposed German unity for centuries.*
    - ▶ *Bismarck adroitly exploited a minor dispute between France and Prussia over the search for a new Spanish monarch. By skillfully editing the Ems Dispatch, Bismarck inflamed relations between France and Prussia.*
    - ▶ *Napoleon III declared war on Prussia on July 19, 1870.*

2. The war
    - ▶ *The Prussians successfully invaded France and forced Napoleon III to surrender on September 2, 1870.*
    - ▶ *On January 18, 1871, King William I was proclaimed German emperor in the Hall of Mirrors at the Palace of Versailles.*

3. The consequences
    - ▶ *Bismarck imposed a harsh settlement. He forced France to pay a huge indemnity and cede Alsace and most of Lorraine to the German empire.*
    - ▶ *The loss of rich deposits of coal and iron ore was a severe blow to France's economy. The loss of these provinces was an even greater blow to French national pride.*
    - ▶ *The unification of Germany created a new European balance of power. As the German empire rapidly industrialized, it became the strongest state on the continent of Europe and a formidable rival to Great Britain.*

VI. THE AUSTRIAN EMPIRE

A. DEFEAT AND DISCONTENT

1. Austria suffered humiliating military defeats at the hands of first France and Piedmont and then Prussia.
2. The empire's biggest problem was the discontent of the many nationalities living under Habsburg rule.

3. The Magyars were the largest and most restive national group.

B. THE DUAL MONARCHY

1. In 1867, Austria agreed to satisfy the Magyars' demands for independence by creating a dual monarchy.
2. Austria and Hungary became independent and equal states under a common Habsburg ruler. The two states still had a united army and a common foreign policy. The new empire was known as Austria-Hungary.

C. CONTINUED SLAVIC DISCONTENT

1. The dual monarchy satisfied the Magyars but failed to solve the empire's nationality problem.
2. The Slavic regions called for but failed to receive a triple monarchy.
3. Slavic discontent posed a significant threat to the future of Austria-Hungary and the peace of Europe.

VII. GREAT BRITAIN: PROSPERITY AND REFORM

A. THE "WORKSHOP OF THE WORLD"

1. Great Britain continued to enjoy unprecedented prosperity.
2. British shipyards led the world in the construction of iron ships.
3. British bankers invested surplus capital in projects all over the globe.

B. THE REFORM BILL OF 1867

1. Britain's rapidly growing working class continued to demand electoral reform.
2. Led by Benjamin Disraeli, the Conservatives (formerly the Tories), supported a new reform bill.
3. The Reform Bill of 1867 extended the suffrage to most of Great Britain's urban workers.

4. It is important to note that British women were still denied the right to vote.

VIII. REALISM IN LITERATURE AND ART

A. KEY CHARACTERISTICS

1. Disenchanted with romanticism
2. Focused on the daily concerns of real people such as workers and peasants
3. Criticized the cruelty of industrial life and the greed and insensitivity of the wealthy

B. LEADING REALIST AUTHORS

1. Charles Dickens, *Hard Times*
2. Gustave Flaubert, *Madame Bovary*
3. Henrik Ibsen, *A Doll's House*
4. Fyodor Dostoyevsky, *Crime and Punishment*

C. LEADING REALIST ARTISTS

1. Gustave Courbet, *The Stonebreakers*
2. Honoré Daumier, *The Third-Class Carriage*
3. Edouard Manet, *Olympia*

Industry, Mass Politics, and Culture, 1871–1914

I. THE SECOND INDUSTRIAL REVOLUTION

A. NEW INDUSTRIES

1. The Bessemer process increased steel production while reducing costs. By 1900, steel had replaced iron in machinery, ships, railroad tracks, and building construction.
2. Led by Germany, the chemical industry grew rapidly. New products included soaps, dyes, fertilizers, and explosives.

B. NEW SOURCES OF POWER

1. Coal and steam gave way to electricity, oil, and gasoline.
2. Electricity proved to be especially versatile. It lit homes and powered everything from industrial machinery to the new streetcars.

C. NEW FORMS OF COMMUNICATION AND TRANSPORTATION

1. First demonstrated by Alexander Graham Bell in 1876, the telephone quickly became an essential part of modern life.
2. The invention of the internal combustion engine enabled mechanics to build gasoline-powered automobiles.

D. NEW INDUSTRIAL POWERS

1. Although Great Britain continued to be a major industrial power, its rate of growth slowed.
2. Germany and the United States emerged as new and formidable industrial rivals.

3. Germany's emergence as Europe's leading industrial power altered the European balance of power, posing a challenge to Great Britain's political and economic leadership.

II. POPULATION GROWTH AND URBANIZATION

A. POPULATION GROWTH

1. As a result of falling death rates and improved agricultural and industrial production, Europe's population rose from 193 million in 1800 to 423 million in 1900.
2. In 1900, Europeans comprised 24 percent of the world's population. The figure today is just 12 percent.

B. URBANIZATION

1. During the nineteenth century, rural people left their villages and crowded into urban tenements.
2. By 1914, the urban population reached 80 percent in Britain, 60 percent in Germany, and 45 percent in France.

III. WOMEN'S RIGHTS

A. KEY VOICES

1. Olympia de Gouges (1748–1793)
   ▸ *French playwright, political activist, and early feminist*
   ▸ *Wrote the* Declaration of the Rights of Woman and of the Female Citizen, *1789*
   ▸ *Demanded that French women be given the same rights as French men*
2. Mary Wollstonecraft (1759–1797)
   ▸ *English author and early feminist*
   ▸ *Wrote* A Vindication of the Rights of Women, *1792*
   ▸ *Argued that women are not naturally inferior to men. They only appear to be inferior because of a lack of education.*

3. John Stuart Mill (1806–1873)
   ▶ *English reformer, essayist, and influential Utilitarian*
   ▶ *Wrote* The Subjection of Women, *1869*
   ▶ *Opposed the social and legal inequalities imposed on women. Argued that inequalities were a relic from the past and "a hindrance to human development."*
4. Henrik Ibsen (1828–1906)
   ▶ *Norwegian playwright and social critic*
   ▶ *Wrote* A Doll's House, *1879*
   ▶ *Criticized conventional marriage roles*

Test Tip *The struggle for women's rights is a very important topic. Be sure that you can identify each of the four authors listed above. Each has generated one or more multiple-choice questions.*

B. "THE ANGEL IN THE HOUSE"

1. The ideal middle-class woman was an "angel in the house." Her most important role was to be the family's moral guardian.
2. Middle-class women were expected to supervise the domestics, manage the household, and direct the children's education.
3. Rising standards of living made it possible for men and women to marry at a younger age. At the same time, the rising cost of child-rearing caused a decline in the size of middle-class families.

C. ECONOMIC CHANGES

1. It is important to remember that most working women were single. Few married women worked outside the home.
2. By the mid-1850s, women and children comprised half of the labor force in the cotton industry. Women were paid about half of a man's wages for similar work.

3. Opportunities for well-educated women were limited to teaching, nursing, and social work.

4. After 1800, many working-class women worked as clerks, typists, and telephone operators.

D. THE STRUGGLE FOR LEGAL AND POLITICAL RIGHTS

1. Law codes in most European countries gave women few legal rights.

2. Divorce was legalized in Britain in 1857 and in France in 1884. However, Catholic countries such as Spain and Italy did not permit divorce.

3. Although the women's suffrage movement commanded wide attention, it achieved few successes. In 1900, no country in Europe allowed women to vote.

E. THE "NEW WOMAN"

1. By the end of the nineteenth century, educated middle-class women enjoyed more independent lifestyles.

2. The "new woman" wore fewer petticoats, often supported herself, and enjoyed sports.

THE AGE OF MASS POLITICS

A. KEY TRENDS

1. Universal male suffrage
   - ▸ *Between 1871 and 1914, most European countries extended the franchise to working-class men.*
   - ▸ *Universal male suffrage led to the creation of mass political parties.*

2. Trade unions and socialist parties
   - ▸ *Trade unions gained rights and played an increasingly important role in Great Britain, France, and Germany.*
   - ▸ *Workers supported socialist political parties in many European countries.*

3. The welfare state
   ‣ *Demands for reform by socialist parties and labor unions persuaded European governments to begin enacting legislation to help the lower classes. These programs laid the foundation for the welfare state.*
   ‣ *It is important to note that a desire to counter the growing strength of socialist parties motivated many of the reforms.*

B. FRANCE

1. The Paris Commune, 1871
   ‣ *The Franco-Prussian War left France defeated and humiliated. France's Third Republic began with the bitter task of ceding the provinces of Alsace and Lorraine to Germany.*
   ‣ *The people of Paris rejected both the treaty and the new conservative government. Radicals called Communards formed a revolutionary municipal council or "Commune."*
   ‣ *Government troops besieged Paris for two months. The army finally overwhelmed the Communards and mercilessly crushed all opposition.*
   ‣ *The bloody suppression of the Paris Commune left a legacy of class hatred that poisoned French politics.*

2. The Dreyfus Affair
   ‣ *Captain Alfred Dreyfus, the first Jewish officer in the French general staff, was convicted of selling military secrets to the Germans and sentenced to life imprisonment on Devil's Island off the northern coast of South America.*
   ‣ *Although Dreyfus was innocent, a coalition of Catholics, monarchists, anti-Semites, and military officers thwarted attempts to clear his name.*
   ‣ *Emile Zola, the famed realist novelist, wrote an article called "J'Accuse" ("I Accuse"), charging that military judges had knowingly let the guilty party go, while Dreyfus remained imprisoned.*

▸ *Dreyfus was ultimately completely exonerated in 1906.*

▸ *The Dreyfus Affair had a number of consequences. It created a nationwide furor that deepened political divisions and revealed widespread anti-Semitism. The Dreyfus Affair also played a key role in Theodor Herzl's decision to write* The Jewish State, *calling for a national homeland for the Jewish people.*

Test Tip

The Dreyfus Affair has generated a significant number of multiple-choice and free-response questions on the APEURO exam. Do not neglect Emile Zola's key role in exposing injustice. You should also be able to discuss the causes and consequences of the Dreyfus Affair and place it in the context of European anti-Semitism.

C. GREAT BRITAIN

1. The Irish Question

   ▸ *Following the Act of Union in 1801, Ireland was united with Great Britain and governed by the British Parliament.*

   ▸ *Led by Charles Parnell, Irish nationalists sought to achieve home rule granting Ireland its own parliament.*

   ▸ *Prime Minister William Gladstone supported Irish home rule. However, a coalition of Conservatives and anti-home-rule Liberals defeated his home rule bills in 1886 and 1892. Gladstone's support for Irish home rule split the Liberal Party, enabling the Conservatives to take power.*

   ▸ *Parliament finally passed an Irish home-rule bill in 1914. However, the British government suspended the bill for the duration of World War I.*

2. Peaceful reforms

   ▸ *The Franchise Act of 1884 extended voting rights to rural male laborers. By 1914, 80 percent of Britain's male population was enfranchised.*

▶ *Parliament laid the foundation for the British welfare state by establishing a system of health and unemployment insurance.*

D. GERMANY

1. Social welfare programs
   - ▶ *During the 1880s, Germany became the first European country to develop a state social welfare program.*
   - ▶ *Otto von Bismarck's social welfare legislation included programs for health insurance, accident insurance, and a system of old-age and disability pensions.*
   - ▶ *Bismarck wanted to prove that the state was a benevolent institution and not an oppressor. He hoped that his social welfare programs would secure the loyalty of workers to the new German empire.*

2. William II (reigned 1888–1918)
   - ▶ *William I died in 1888 at the age of 90. His grandson, William II, became the new German kaiser. Arrogant and impulsive, William II was determined to rule on his own.*
   - ▶ *William II forced Bismarck to resign in 1890. During the next 14 years, he expanded Bismarck's social reforms. At same time, Germany's economic and military power continued to grow.*

E. RUSSIA

1. Autocracy and repression
   - ▶ *The assassination of Tsar Alexander II ended Russia's brief period of reform.*
   - ▶ *Both Alexander III (reigned 1881–1894) and Nicholas II (reigned 1894–1917) were committed to the traditional policies of autocracy, orthodoxy, and Russification.*
   - ▶ *Both tsars encouraged anti-Semitic attacks on Jews. Russia was the last European state to eliminate legal discrimination against Jews.*

2. Political movements
   - ▶ *Russia's program of rapid industrialization spawned a wide range of political movements.*

> ▶ *The Constitutional Democrats or Kadets wanted a constitutional monarchy.*
> ▶ *The Social Democrats worked for economic and political revolution. In 1903, the Social Democrats split into two factions. The Mensheviks favored gradual socialistic reform. Led by Vladimir Lenin, the Bolsheviks advocated a communist revolution spearheaded by a small elite of professional revolutionaries.*

3. The Revolution of 1905

> ▶ *Russian losses in the Russo-Japanese War exposed the weaknesses of the autocratic regime and led to increased unrest.*
> ▶ *On January 22, 1905, Cossacks opened fire on a peaceful crowd of workers outside the Winter Palace in St. Petersburg. The "Bloody Sunday" massacre provoked a wave of strikes and demands for change.*
> ▶ *Nicholas II reluctantly approved the election of a Russian parliament or Duma.*
> ▶ *Nicholas stubbornly refused to work with the Duma, insisting that it become an advisory rather than a legislative body.*

V. SCIENCE AND THE AGE OF PROGRESS

A. THE BACTERIAL REVOLUTION

1. Louis Pasteur

> ▶ *Conducted experiments that supported the germ theory of diseases*
> ▶ *Discovered that heat could destroy many harmful bacteria*

2. Robert Koch

> ▶ *Identified the bacteria responsible for specific diseases*
> ▶ *Identified the tuberculosis bacteria*

3. Joseph Lister

> ▶ *Promoted the idea of sterile surgery*
> ▶ *Introduced carbolic acid to sterilize surgical instruments and wounds*

4. Impact
  ▸ *The bacterial revolution saved millions of lives, thus causing a dramatic decline in European death rates.*
  ▸ *Urban residents benefited the most from improvement in public health.*

B. CHARLES DARWIN AND THE THEORY OF EVOLUTION

1. The Origin of Species
  ▸ *Darwin was a British biologist.*
  ▸ *His watershed book,* The Origin of Species, *challenged the idea of special creation by proposing a revolutionary theory of biological evolution.*

2. Key points
  ▸ *Informed by Thomas Malthus's Essay on Population, Darwin concluded that every living plant and animal takes part in a constant "struggle for existence."*
  ▸ *Only the "fittest" species survive this struggle.*
  ▸ *The fittest are determined by a process of natural selection in which new species emerge after gradually accumulating new modifications.*

C. SOCIAL DARWINISM

1. Herbert Spencer, an English sociologist, applied Darwin's theories to human society. Spencer argued that free economic competition was natural selection in action. The best companies make profits while inefficient ones go bankrupt. The same rules also apply to individuals.
2. Wealthy business and industrial leaders used social Darwinism to justify their success and oppose social welfare programs.
3. Social Darwinists also applied the theories of natural selection and survival of the fittest to races and nations. Their theories helped rationalize and justify imperialism, racism, and militarism.

VI. **MODERN ART**

A. MODERNITY

1. New inventions such as the camera and the cinema posed a challenge to how artists traditionally portrayed people and places.
2. Artists responded with a variety of "modern" styles that marked a break with long-standing artistic traditions.

B. IMPRESSIONISM

1. Key characteristics
   ▶ *Captured a moment in time; a slice of life*
   ▶ *Interested in the fleeting effects of light on color*
   ▶ *Depicted leisure activities of the Parisian bourgeoisie*
2. Key artists and works
   ▶ *Claude Monet,* Impression Sunrise, Gare St.-Lazare
   ▶ *Pierre-Auguste Renoir,* Le Bal au Moulin de la Galette, Luncheon of the Boating Party

C. CUBISM

1. Key characteristics
   ▶ *Presented multiple views of the same object*
   ▶ *Fragmented forms into flat, jagged shapes*
   ▶ *Portrayed flat, two-dimensional space without traditional linear perspective*
2. Key artists and works
   ▶ *Pablo Picasso,* Les Demoiselles d'Avignon, Guernica
   ▶ *Georges Braque,* Violin and Candlestick

D. <u>MAKING COMPARISONS:</u> RAPHAEL AND PICASSO

1. Raphael's *School of Athens*
   ▶ *Demonstrates the humanist interest in Greek and Roman philosophy*
   ▶ *Utilizes the Renaissance artistic techniques of idealized human portraits and linear perspective*

▸ *Exhibits harmony, proportion, and balance*
▸ *Painted for Pope Julius II, illustrating the importance of church patronage*

2. Picasso's *Les Demoiselles d'Avignon*

▸ *Demonstrates the modernist interest in the ugly underside of real life by depicting five prostitutes inside a brothel*
▸ *Utilizes the Cubist artistic techniques of flat forms, fragmented space, and multiple views of the same person*
▸ *Exhibits a lack of harmony and proportion*
▸ *Painted for a limited group of artists, dealers, and critics*

War and Revolution

I. IMPERIALISM

A. OLD IMPERIALISM AND THE NEW IMPERIALISM

1. Old imperialism
    - ▶ *European powers had practiced a form of imperialism between the sixteenth and seventeenth centuries. During this period, Portugal, the Dutch Republic, and England built trading post empires along the coasts of Africa, India, and Indonesia.*
    - ▶ *The New World was a notable exception to this pattern. Spain established an enormous empire in Central and South America while England colonized the east coast of North America.*

2. New imperialism
    - ▶ *Beginning in 1870, European nations exercised increasing economic and political control over Africa and Asia. No longer content to trade with other peoples, European nations now aimed to directly rule vast regions of the world.*
    - ▶ *The imperialist powers seized control over some areas such as German East Africa and French Indo-China. In other areas, they established protectorates where the dependent country had its own government but was still subject to the authority of the imperial power. And finally, the great powers established spheres of influence over large parts of China.*

B. MOTIVES FOR THE NEW IMPERIALISM

1. Industrialists searched for new sources of raw materials and new markets for their finished goods.
2. Militarists and nationalists sought power and prestige.
3. Social Darwinists believed that strong nations had a natural right to dominate weaker peoples.
4. Missionaries believed that Europeans had a duty to undertake a "civilizing mission" to bring Christianity and the blessings of advanced technology to less fortunate people.

C. THE "SCRAMBLE FOR AFRICA"

1. The most aggressive example of the new imperialism took place in Africa.
2. The so-called "Scramble for Africa" became so frenetic and rapacious that Otto von Bismarck (see Chapter 17) called for an international conference in Berlin. The 14 nations that attended the 1885 Berlin Conference established rules for dividing Africa.
3. Led by Great Britain, France, and Germany, the European powers successfully partitioned almost the entire continent of Africa. Only Liberia and Abyssinia (Ethiopia) remained independent.

D. CONSEQUENCES OF THE NEW IMPERIALISM

1. Damaged and sometimes destroyed native cultures
2. Created a global economy
3. Intensified European rivalries

II. THE MARCH TO WAR

A. GERMANY AND THE NEW BALANCE OF POWER

1. Germany's industrial capacity, population, and military power all dramatically increased. In 1900, Germany produced more steel than Great Britain and France combined. Germany's population increased from 41 million in 1871 to 64 million in 1910. In contrast, France had just 40 million people in 1910.

2. European leaders from Cardinal Richelieu (see chapter 9) to Prince Klemens von Metternich (see chapter 15) had feared a united Germany. Their fears now became a reality. As Germany's power surged, its leaders demanded respect and a new "place in the sun."

B. BISMARCK'S NETWORK OF ALLIANCES

1. The French were humiliated by their defeat in the Franco-Prussian War and embittered by their loss of Alsace-Lorraine.
2. In an attempt to isolate France, Bismarck formed a military alliance with Austria-Hungary in 1879. Three years later, Italy joined these two countries, thus forming the Triple Alliance.
3. In 1887, Bismarck took yet another ally away from France by signing a treaty with Russia.

C. WILLIAM II'S AGGRESSIVE POLICIES

1. In 1890, Kaiser William II forced Bismarck to resign.
2. William II promptly set Germany on a new course by letting the treaty of friendship with Russia lapse.
3. William II then challenged Britain's long-standing naval supremacy by embarking on an expensive program of naval expansion that poisoned relations between the two countries.

D. THE FORMATION OF THE TRIPLE ENTENTE

1. France immediately offered Russia financial investments and diplomatic friendship. The two nations signed a Franco-Russian Alliance in 1894.
2. Alarmed by Germany's growing naval power, Britain abandoned its policy of "splendid isolation." In 1904, Britain concluded a series of agreements with France collectively called the Entente Cordiale. With French support, the British concluded a similar agreement with Russia, thus forming the Triple Entente.
3. Germany tested the Anglo-French entente by challenging France's plan to dominate Morocco. However, Germany's belligerent actions only served to draw France and Britain closer together.

CHRONOLOGICAL REVIEW

4. Two rival alliances now confronted each other. A dispute between any two powers could easily escalate into a major war.

E. THE BALKAN POWDER KEG

1. As the power of the Ottoman Empire receded, the Balkan Peninsula became a powder keg of competing interests.

2. With the exception of the Greeks and the Romanians, most of the Balkan population spoke the same Slavic language. Many Slavs embraced Pan-Slavism, a nationalist movement to unite all Slavic peoples.

3. Bismarck recognized the potential danger of nationalist aspirations in the Balkans. At the 1878 Congress of Berlin, he tried to reduce tensions by supporting Serbian independence and Austria-Hungary's right to "occupy and administer" Bosnia and Herzegovina.

4. The newly independent nation of Serbia quickly became the leader of the Pan-Slavic movement. Serbian leaders hoped to unite the Slavs in the same way Piedmont had united the Italians and Prussia the Germans.

5. Austria felt threatened by the growth of Slavic nationalism within its borders and across the Balkans. In 1908, the Austrians enraged the Serbs by annexing Bosnia and Herzegovina.

6. Serbian nationalism threatened Austria. At the same time, it offered Slavic Russia an opportunity to advance its interests in the Balkans.

7. Russia and Austria-Hungary were thus on a collision course in the Balkans. As one Balkan crisis followed another, Europe tottered on the brink of war.

F. THE OUTBREAK OF WAR

1. On June 28, 1914, a 19-year-old Slav nationalist, Gavrilo Princip, assassinated Archduke Francis Ferdinand, the heir to the Austrian throne.

2. The assassination set in motion a sequence of events that plunged Europe into war. In August 1914, millions of soldiers marched off to battle, convinced the war would be over in a few weeks.

AP European textbooks devote lengthy discussions to the complex sequence of events that led to the outbreak of World War I. Interestingly, APEURO test writers devote very few multiple-choice questions to this topic. Don't become bogged down trying to memorize the details of the Balkan wars and the exchange of ultimatums between the Great Powers. Devote the majority of your time to studying the consequences of World War I for the home front, for Russia, and for postwar Europe.

III. THE WAR IN THE WEST

A. THE SCHLIEFFEN PLAN

1. Germany faced the daunting task of simultaneously fighting France on its western border and Russia along a lengthy eastern front.

2. In order to prevent a two-front war, General Alfred von Schlieffen drew up a master plan calling for an all-out attack against France. The Schlieffen Plan gambled that France could be knocked out of the war before Russia had a chance to fully mobilize its forces.

3. A lightning attack on France meant invading neutral Belgium.

4. Germany's unprovoked attack on Belgium outraged Britain. On August 4, 1914, Britain declared war on Germany.

B. STALEMATE

1. The Schlieffen Plan narrowly failed, making a quick victory impossible.

2. Both sides now constructed an elaborate system of trenches stretching more than 600 miles from the English Channel to the Swiss border.

3. Trench warfare produced a stalemate that lasted about four years and claimed unprecedented casualities.

C. THE HOME FRONT

1. Total war

   ▸ *When it became clear that the war would not be over quickly, governments mobilized all human and industrial resources in order to wage total war.*

   ▸ *Governments tightly controlled the news and used propaganda to rally public morale and arouse hatred of the enemy.*

2. The role of women

   ▸ *As more and more men went to war, millions of women replaced them in factories, offices, and shops. World War I marked the first time that the employment of women was essential to a sustained war effort.*

   ▸ *In the decade prior to World War I, British women led by Emmeline Pankhurst waged an aggressive campaign for women's suffrage. During the war, Pankhurst called a halt to militant suffrage activities, urging women to contribute to the war effort.*

   ▸ *In 1918, Parliament granted the suffrage to women over the age of 30.*

D. *ALL QUIET ON THE WESTERN FRONT*

1. *All Quiet on the Western Front* is a war novel written by Erich Maria Remarque, a German veteran of World War I.

2. Remarque vividly described the senseless slaughter and suffering endured by soldiers on the Western Front.

IV. THE RUSSIAN REVOLUTION

A. THE END OF ROMANOV RULE

1. The poorly equipped Russian army was no match for the German war machine. By 1917, more than 7 million Russian soldiers had been killed, wounded, or taken prisoner.

2. Nicholas II proved to be an inept ruler. As battlefield losses mounted and shortages of food worsened, Nicholas moved his headquarters to the front in a futile attempt to rally his troops.

3. In early 1917, food shortages in Petrograd (formerly St. Petersburg) led to spontaneous demonstrations and strikes.

4. Nicholas ordered his troops to restore order, but the soldiers refused and instead supported the demonstrators. On March 12, 1917, Nicholas II abdicated, ending three centuries of Romanov rule.

B. THE PROVISIONAL GOVERNMENT

1. A provisional government led by Alexander Kerensky replaced the tsar.

2. Despite mounting losses, the provisional government continued the war against Germany. This fateful decision to pursue an unpopular war weakened the provisional government and played a key role in its demise.

C. VLADIMIR LENIN AND THE BOLSHEVIK REVOLUTION

1. While the Russian army was falling apart, the Germans helped Lenin return to Petrograd. Lenin arrived at the Finland Station on April 3, 1917, and promptly urged his followers to overthrow the provisional government.

2. Lenin's key ideas
   ▸ *Lenin denounced gradual reform, arguing that capitalism could only be destroyed by class conflict.*
   ▸ *Lenin insisted that a communist revolution was possible in a nonindustrialized country such as Russia.*
   ▸ *Lenin argued that Russia's relatively small working class could not develop a revolutionary class consciousness. Instead, leadership would have to come from a highly disciplined group of professional revolutionaries.*

3. Lenin's slogan of "Peace, Land, and Bread" captured the popular imagination and enabled the Bolsheviks to win widespread popular support.

4. Lenin sensed that it was time to act. "History will not forgive us," Lenin wrote, "if we do not seize power now." On the night of November 6, 1917, the Bolsheviks occupied most government buildings. The next day Lenin proclaimed establishment of a new Bolshevik government.

D. THE TREATY OF BREST-LITOVSK

1. Lenin realized that the survival of the Bolshevik regime depended upon ending the war with Germany.
2. In March 1918, the Bolsheviks reluctantly agreed to the Treaty of Brest-Litovsk. Under the terms of this treaty, Russia lost a quarter of its European territory and a third of its population.
3. It is important to note that Russia later repudiated the treaty, and it was declared null and void by the Allies.

E. CIVIL WAR

1. By the summer of 1918, several "White" armies attempted to overthrow the Bolsheviks.
2. Led by Leon Trotsky, the Bolsheviks responded by forming a highly disciplined Red Army.
3. The civil war between the Whites and the Reds lasted from 1918 to 1920. The divided and poorly led Whites lost to the better-organized Red Army.

Test Tip

Lenin's pivotal role in the Russian Revolution has generated a significant number of multiple-choice questions on the APEURO exam. Be sure you study Lenin's key ideas. It is interesting to compare Lenin's decisive leadership with the weakness and vacillation of Tsar Nicholas II and Alexander Kerensky.

V. THE PEACE SETTLEMENT

A. THE END OF WORLD WAR I

1. The Treaty of Brest-Litovsk enabled the Germans to transfer divisions from the east to help launch a great spring offensive.
2. Reinforced by newly arrived American troops, the British and French halted the German offensive.
3. Realizing that defeat was imminent, William II abdicated his throne and Germany became a republic. Two days later on November 11, 1918, World War I came to an end.

B. THE FOURTEEN POINTS

1. President Woodrow Wilson became the spokesman for a just and lasting peace.
2. Wilson's Fourteen Points included a call for the following:
    - ▶ *Open diplomacy*
    - ▶ *Freedom of the seas*
    - ▶ *Reduction of national armaments*
    - ▶ *Return of Alsace-Lorraine to France*
    - ▶ *A free and independent Poland with access to the sea*
    - ▶ *National self-determination for oppressed minority groups*
    - ▶ *Creation of a "general association of nations" to preserve the peace and security of its members*
3. Wilson's idealistic proposals were undermined by secret treaties and by a desire to punish Germany.

C. THE PARIS PEACE CONFERENCE

1. Although nearly 30 countries were represented, Great Britain, France, and the United States made the major decisions.
2. Germany and Austria-Hungary were not allowed to attend the conference.
3. Russia, which had suffered the greatest loss of life, was in the midst of a civil war and was not invited to attend the conference.

D. THE TREATY OF VERSAILLES

1. Germany lost 13 percent of its land, including Alsace-Lorraine.
2. Germany's territories in Africa and the Pacific were given as mandates to Britain, France, and Japan. A mandate was a territory that was administered on behalf of the League of Nations.
3. Poland once again became an independent nation. The new Poland received a large strip of German land called the Polish Corridor. This strip cut off East Prussia from the rest of Germany and gave Poland access to the sea.

4. Germany's army was limited to 100,000 men and forbidden to have artillery, aircraft, or submarines.

5. The east bank of the Rhine River was to be demilitarized, and the Allies were to have the right to occupy the Rhineland for 15 years.

6. Germany was declared guilty of starting the war and forced to pay huge payments called reparations.

7. The Allies created a League of Nations to discuss and settle disputes without resorting to war.

8. The final signing ceremony took place in the Hall of Mirrors at Versailles, the same room in which Bismarck's German empire had been proclaimed in 1871.

E. A NEW MAP OF EUROPE

1. Austria-Hungary was dissolved and the Habsburg monarchy eliminated. Austria and Hungary became separate states. In addition, territories from Austria-Hungary were given to the newly created states of Czechoslovakia and Yugoslavia.

2. The Serbs dominated Yugoslavia.

3. Finland and the three Baltic states—Estonia, Latvia, and Lithuania—emerged from the tsarist empire.

F. MAKING COMPARISONS: THE CONGRESS OF VIENNA AND THE PARIS PEACE CONFERENCE

1. The Congress of Vienna
   - *Allowed defeated France to participate in peace conference negotiations*
   - *Established a framework for future international relations based on periodic meetings, or congresses, among the great powers*
   - *Restored a conservative order based upon the institutions of monarchy and aristocracy*
   - *Created a balance of power that lasted for over 50 years*

2. The Paris Peace Conference
   ▶ *Refused to allow defeated Germany or Communist Russia to participate in peace conference negotiations*
   ▶ *Established a framework for future international relations based on the League of Nations*
   ▶ *Witnessed the birth of a democratic order with the elimination of monarchies in Germany, Austria-Hungary, and Russia*
   ▶ *Created a legacy of bitterness between both the victors and the defeated, which led to a second world war in just 20 years*

CHRONOLOGICAL REVIEW

The Age of Anxiety

I. THE INTELLECTUAL CRISIS

A. OLD CERTAINTIES

1. Belief in the power of reason to understand the universe and discover natural laws.
2. Belief in progress and the power of science and technology to improve living standards.
3. Belief in liberty and the power of individual rights to promote a just society.

B. THE IMPACT OF WORLD WAR I

1. Caused unprecedented death and destruction
2. Overthrew established monarchies and social orders in Russia, Germany, and Austria-Hungary
3. Led many people to question the optimistic belief in reason, progress, and individual rights

C. THE TERRIBLE UNCERTAINTIES

1. A widespread feeling of disillusionment, uncertainty, and anxiety
2. New doubts about the ability of individuals to control their lives
3. An intellectual crisis that affected every field of thought

II. MODERN PHILOSOPHY

A. FRIEDRICH NIETZSCHE (1844–1900)

1. Considered an important forerunner of existentialism
2. Expressed contempt for middle-class morality, saying that it led to a false and shallow existence
3. Argued that conventional notions of good and evil are only relevant for the ordinary person
4. Rejected reason and embraced the irrational
5. Believed that the "will-to-power" of a few heroic "supermen" could successfully reorder the world

B. EXISTENTIALISM: KEY IDEAS

1. Reason and science are incapable of providing insight into the human situation.
2. God, reason, and progress are myths; humans live in a hostile world, alone and isolated.
3. This condition of loneliness is a challenge and a call to action. Men and women give meaning to their lives through their choices. A person is therefore the sum of his or her actions and choices.

C. EXISTENTIALISM: KEY THINKERS

1. Jean-Paul Sartre, *Being and Nothingness*
2. Albert Camus, *The Stranger*

III. The New Physics

A. NEWTONIAN PHYSICS

1. From the time of Isaac Newton to the early twentieth century, physical scientists believed that unchanging natural laws governed the universe.
2. This mechanistic view of nature supported an optimistic belief in progress toward what one researcher called "a boundless future."

B. ALBERT EINSTEIN (1879–1955)

1. Theories
   - ▶ *Einstein proposed his special theory of relativity in 1905. He challenged traditional conceptions of time, space, and motion.*
   - ▶ *His famous equation $E = mc^2$ (energy = mass × the square of the speed of light) declared that mass and energy are interchangeable. This discovery laid the foundation for the development of nuclear power.*

2. Implications
   - ▶ *Instead of living in a rational world with few uncertainties, humans lived in a new universe with few certainties. Everything was "relative" or dependent on the observer's frame of reference.*
   - ▶ *It is important to note that Einstein's theories did not immediately affect the average person's outlook on life. However, intellectuals and popular writers realized that by pulling the rug out from under perceived reality, the new physics contributed to the uncertainties of the postwar world.*

It is very important to remember that APEURO is not AP Physics. You will not be asked to explain the complexities of Einstein's theories. You will be expected to know that the new physics challenged traditional notions of causality, time, and space. It undermined the optimistic confidence that people lived in a predictable and orderly world.

IV. THE NEW PSYCHOLOGY

A. BEFORE FREUD

1. Romantic artists and authors had explored the inner worlds of emotion and imagination.
2. Professional psychologists assumed that human behavior was based upon rational decisions by the conscious mind.

CHRONOLOGICAL REVIEW

B. SIGMUND FREUD (1856–1939)

1. Theories

▸ *Freud believed that the human psyche includes three distinct parts, which he called the id, the superego, and the ego.*

▸ *The id consists of inborn sexual and aggressive urges.*

▸ *The superego acts as the conscience that seeks to repress the id. It develops as children learn their culture's moral values.*

▸ *When the superego checks the pleasure-seeking impulses of the id, it drives them into the realm of the subconscious mind. The subconscious is irrational and recognizes no ethical restrictions.*

▸ *The ego is the center of reason. It attempts to find a balance between the conflicting demands of the id and the superego.*

2. Implications

▸ *Freud's theories undermined the Enlightenment's belief that humans are fundamentally rational beings. Instead, humans are irrational beings capable of destroying themselves and society.*

▸ *Freud's emphasis upon the power of uncontrolled irrational and unconscious drives provided an unsettling explanation for the seemingly incomprehensible horrors unleashed by World War I.*

▸ *Freud's studies of the world of the unconscious mind had a significant influence on modern art and literature.*

V. MODERN ART, ARCHITECTURE, AND LITERATURE

A. SURREALISM

1. Key characteristics

▸ *Depicts the world of the unconscious mind as revealed in dreams and fantasies*

▸ *Reveals the influence of Freudian psychology*

▸ *Portrays strange objects and symbols that express the artist's inner mind*

2. Key artists and works
- ▸ *Giorgio de Chirico,* The Song of Love
- ▸ *Salvador Dali,* The Persistence of Memory

B. BAUHAUS ARCHITECTURE

1. Key characteristics
   - ▸ *Architecture should be practical, useful, and above all, functional.*
   - ▸ *Architects should avoid using unnecessary exterior decorations and instead rely on clear straight lines.*
   - ▸ *Builders should use modern materials and support materials including glass, steel, ferroconcrete, and cantilevers.*
   - ▸ *It is important to note that the Bauhaus style originated in Germany and spread to the United States where it became known as the International Style.*
2. Key architects and buildings
   - ▸ *Walter Gropius,* The Fagus Shoe Factory, Bauhaus workshop wing
   - ▸ *Le Corbusier,* Villa Savoye

C. TWENTIETH-CENTURY LITERATURE

1. Key characteristics
   - ▸ *Questions accepted values and practices*
   - ▸ *Expresses discontent and alienation from middle-class conformity and materialism*
   - ▸ *Focuses on the complexity and irrationality of the human mind*
   - ▸ *Employs the stream-of-consciousness technique to explore the human psyche*
2. Key authors and works
   - ▸ *James Joyce,* Ulysses
   - ▸ *Marcel Proust,* Remembrance of Things Past
   - ▸ *William Faulkner,* The Sound and the Fury
   - ▸ *T. S. Eliot,* The Waste Land

VI. THE SEARCH FOR A STABLE INTERNATIONAL ORDER

A. PROBLEMS

1. Germany resented the Versailles Treaty's harsh terms, calling it a *Diktat*, or imposed settlement.
2. The United States rejected the Versailles Treaty and followed a policy of isolationism.
3. France was determined to enforce the Versailles Treaty and make Germany pay reparations for the damage it had caused.
4. Communist Russia remained outside the international system.

B. GERMANY: THE WEIMAR REPUBLIC

1. Reparations
   - *The new German republic—generally known as the Weimar Republic—faced staggering reparations payments.*
   - *When the Weimar Republic proposed a three-year moratorium on making reparation payments, the French occupied the Ruhr Valley and seized goods as payments.*
2. Inflation
   - *The Weimar Republic supported itself by printing vast amounts of paper money. By December 1923, one dollar was worth 4 trillion German marks.*
   - *The 1923 inflation destroyed the savings and incomes of the German middle class. Feeling betrayed by their government, embittered Germans would later be susceptible to Nazi propaganda.*

C. HOPE FOR PEACE

1. The Dawes Plan
   - *At the end of 1923, a committee of experts led by American Charles Dawes devised a plan to reestablish a sound German currency and reduce reparation payments.*

▶ *The Dawes Plan provided a series of American loans to Germany. The infusion of American money revitalized the German economy, thus ending the inflationary spiral.*

2. The Locarno Pact

▶ *France, Germany, England, Italy, and Belgium signed the Locarno Pact guaranteeing the borders between Germany and France.*

▶ *The Locarno Pact marked an important turning point in Franco-German relations and appeared to offer the hope of a new era of peaceful relations between these two rivals.*

3. The Kellogg-Briand Pact, 1928

▶ *In 1928, 62 countries including the United States signed a pact promising "to renounce war as an instrument of national policy."*

▶ *At the time, the Kellogg-Briand Pact appeared to bolster collective security and promote a renewed spirit of optimism.*

It is easy to overlook the political events of the 1920s, since they were overturned by the tumultuous and far more famous events of the 1930s. Don't make this mistake. The Dawes Plan, the Locarno Pact, and the Kellogg-Briand Pact have all generated multiple-choice questions. Make sure that you can identify each of these agreements.

Depression, Dictators, and World War II

I. THE GREAT DEPRESSION

A. CAUSES

1. Several long-term problems negatively affected the U.S. economy:
   - ▶ *Companies overproduced consumer goods.*
   - ▶ *Consumers did not have enough money or credit to purchase goods*
   - ▶ *Farmers overproduced agricultural products, driving down prices and incomes.*

2. The American stock market crash caused enormous financial losses and triggered a global financial crisis.

3. Worried American bankers recalled loans to European banks. Austria's largest bank failed, starting a financial panic in central Europe.

4. The financial crisis led to sharp declines in global trade and manufacturing.

5. The United States raised protective tariffs, forcing other nations to retaliate.

6. Governments cut budgets and reduced spending, helping to accelerate the downward economic spiral.

B. IMPACT ON EUROPE

1. Replaced the optimistic spirit of the late 1920s with a growing sense of doubt and fear

2. Created uncertainty and insecurity for millions of unemployed workers

3. Prompted increased government economic intervention
4. Created opportunities for demagogues and dictators to exploit people's fears.

 ## II. CONSERVATIVE AUTHORITARIANISM AND TOTALITARIANISM

A. CONSERVATIVE AUTHORITARIANISM

1. Committed to the existing social order
2. Opposed to popular participation in government
3. Revived in eastern Europe, Spain, and Portugal

B. TOTALITARIANISM

1. Exercised total control over the lives of individual citizens
2. Used modern technology and communication to manipulate and censor information
3. Used education to mold loyal citizens and demonize scapegoats and enemies

C. FORMS OF TOTALITARIANISM

1. Fascism
   - *Led by one leader and one party*
   - *Condemned democracy, arguing that rival parties undermine national unity*
   - *Supported state-sponsored capitalism*
   - *Glorified war and aggressive nationalism*
   - *Exercised control over the media*
2. Communism
   - *Led by one party, the "dictatorship of the proletariat"*
   - *Condemned capitalism, arguing that it exploits workers*
   - *Supported state ownership of the means of production*
   - *Glorified the working class*
   - *Exercised control over the media*

LENIN, STALIN, AND COMMUNIST RUSSIA, 1921–1939

A. VLADIMIR LENIN AND THE NEW ECONOMIC POLICY

1. Widespread famine, a deteriorating economy, and increasing unrest all plagued Russia following the civil war.

2. Lenin pragmatically realized that he needed to make a tactical retreat. In March 1921, he launched the New Economic Policy. It called for a temporary compromise with capitalism. Small businesses were denationalized, and peasants were allowed to establish free markets in agricultural products. The Communist Party still maintained control of large industries such as oil and steel.

3. The New Economic Policy successfully revived the Russian economy. By 1928, the country's farms and factories produced as much as they had before World War I.

B. JOSEPH STALIN VERSUS LEON TROTSKY

1. Lenin's death in 1924 created a power struggle between Trotsky and Stalin.

2. As a charismatic leader since 1905, Trotsky was second only to Lenin in fame. Trotsky believed that Russia should support communist revolutions around the world.

3. In contrast, Stalin was a quiet man who preferred to work behind the scenes. As general secretary of the Communist Party, Stalin placed his supporters in key positions. Stalin argued that communism should first gain a firm hold in Russia before supporting a global revolution.

4. Stalin proved to be cunning and ruthless. He successfully expelled Trotsky from the Communist Party. By 1927, Stalin stood alone as the Soviet Union's undisputed leader.

C. THE FIVE-YEAR PLANS

1. In 1928, Stalin launched the first of a series of five-year plans designed to transform the Soviet Union's economic and social structure. The plans had the following goals:

   ▶ *End the New Economic Policy*

CHRONOLOGICAL REVIEW

> ‣ *Create a socialist command economy in which the government makes all economic decisions*
> ‣ *Promote the rapid development of heavy industries*
> ‣ *Collectivize agriculture*

2. Stalin's commitment to a program of massive, large-scale industrialism produced results. By 1940, the Soviet Union was a major industrial power, trailing only the United States and Germany.

3. Stalin's campaign to collectivize agriculture was less successful. Conservative Russian peasants opposed surrendering their land and joining a collective farm. Stalin denounced resisting peasants as kulaks and ordered party officials to "liquidate them as a class." Kulaks and other peasants were executed, starved, and deported to forced-labor camps.

D. THE GREAT TERROR

1. Stalin was a totalitarian dictator who was more powerful than the most autocratic tsar.

2. During the mid-1930s, Stalin launched a program of state-sponsored terror that began with show trials to eliminate Old Bolsheviks. The Great Terror expanded to include intellectuals, army officers, party members, and ordinary citizens.

3. At least 8 million people were arrested. Millions of innocent people died in forced-labor camps called gulags.

E. MAKING COMPARISONS: THE REIGN OF TERROR AND THE GREAT TERROR

1. The Reign of Terror, 1793–1794

> ‣ *Ordered by the Committee of Public Safety led by Maximilien Robespierre*
> ‣ *Intended to save the Revolution from foreign and domestic enemies*
> ‣ *Justified by the goal of creating a "republic of virtue" where all citizens would possess high moral standards and be dedicated to the public good*
> ‣ *Eliminated political rivals such as Georges-Jacques Danton*

- ▶ *Failed to create supporters for Robespierre*
- ▶ *Used public executions by the guillotine to terrorize the entire nation*
- ▶ *Ended when the Convention reasserted its authority by arresting and executing Robespierre*

2. The Great Terror, 1934–1938
  - ▶ *Ordered by Joseph Stalin, general secretary of the Communist Party and dictator of the Soviet Union*
  - ▶ *Purged Old Bolsheviks and other political rivals who threatened Stalin's power*
  - ▶ *Justified by claiming the existence of a plot masterminded by Trotsky along with Fascist enemies to overthrow Stalin*
  - ▶ *Used public show trials, executions, and mass imprisonment to terrorize the entire nation*
  - ▶ *Ended when all rivals to Stalin had been eliminated*
  - ▶ *Created a new Communist Party staffed with members who demonstrated total loyalty to Stalin*

IV. MUSSOLINI AND FASCIST ITALY

A. POSTWAR ITALY

1. Italy had entered World War I in hopes of winning mandates in East Africa and Austrian territory along the Adriatic Sea. When the Treaty of Versailles rejected these claims, embittered Italian nationalists felt betrayed.
2. Italy faced a severe economic crisis that included soaring inflation, rising unemployment, and a massive national debt.
3. Italy's upper and middle classes feared that the economic crisis and growing labor unrest might lead to a communist revolt, as had just happened in Russia.

B. THE RISE OF BENITO MUSSOLINI

1. Growing numbers of Italians demanded action and waited impatiently for a strong leader.

2. Mussolini used Italy's political power vacuum to seize power. As the leader of the Fascist Party, he boldly promised to revive Italy's economy and rebuild its armed forces.

3. In 1922, Mussolini called upon his followers to march on Rome. Although the government could have stopped Mussolini with a show of force, King Victor Emmanuel III gave in and named Mussolini prime minister.

C. THE FASCIST STATE

1. Mussolini quickly consolidated his power and organized a Fascist state.

2. Mussolini outlawed all political parties except the Fascists.

3. Mussolini's propaganda encouraged Italians to accept his leadership without question. Slogans such as "Mussolini Is Always Right" covered billboards across Italy.

D. THE CORPORATE ECONOMY

1. Mussolini believed that capitalists and workers must be forced to cooperate for the good of the state.

2. He organized 22 state corporations to run all parts of the Italian economy. Each corporation included employers, employees, and government arbitrators.

3. The corporations outlawed strikes and set wages and prices.

4. It is important to note that Mussolini's corporate state combined private ownership with state control over economic decisions.

E. THE LATERAN ACCORD

1. Mussolini successfully negotiated an end to the long dispute between the papacy and the Italian state.

2. Pope Pius XII recognized the legitimacy of the Italian state. In return, Mussolini recognized Vatican City as an independent state ruled by the pope.

APEURO tests do not devote as much attention to Mussolini as they do to Adolf Hitler and Stalin. Don't be distracted by the Black Shirts, the March on Rome, and Mussolini's bombastic speeches. Instead, focus on the ideology of fascism and the characteristics of Mussolini's corporate state.

V. HITLER AND NAZI GERMANY

A. REASONS WHY THE WEIMAR REPUBLIC FAILED

1. Many Germans refused to believe that their army had been defeated in battle. They believed instead that the German army had been betrayed by socialist and liberal politicians associated with the new Weimar Republic.

2. The Versailles Treaty outraged German nationalists who resented the war-guilt clause and the loss of territory to Poland. Constant nationalist agitation undermined support for the Weimar Republic.

3. Conservatives wanted a strong leader who would restore order and reduce the power of labor unions.

4. Runaway inflation during the early 1920s destroyed middle-class savings, thus eroding confidence in the government.

5. The Great Depression had a particularly devastating impact on Germany. Millions of workers lost faith in the Weimar Republic.

6. Article 48 of the German constitution helped to undermine the republican government by allowing the president to rule by decree in cases of national emergency.

B. REASONS WHY ADOLF HITLER ROSE TO POWER

1. The weakness of the Weimar Republic helped prepare the public for a bold leader who would restore German pride.

2. Hitler concluded that he would not attempt to overthrow the Weimar Republic by revolutionary means. Instead, he would use the electoral process to legally gain power.

3. Hitler was a spellbinding demagogue who denounced the Weimar Republic and the Versailles Treaty. He skillfully used modern propaganda techniques to convince the German people to follow his leadership.

4. Hitler offered the German people an ideology that exploited their fears. The Nazi program included the following key points:

   ▸ *Nationalism: German national honor would be avenged by regaining the lands taken by the Versailles Treaty.*

   ▸ *Master race: the Germans were a master race who needed land in eastern Europe and Russia.*

   ▸ *Anti-Semitism: Jews were an inferior race responsible for many of Germany's problems.*

   ▸ *Anticommunism: Marxists were responsible for fomenting labor unrest. Much of Hitler's anti-Semitism focused on alleged Jewish responsibility for the rise of communism.*

   ▸ *The fuhrer: Parliamentary government produced weak, vacillating politicians. Hitler believed that Germany required an absolute leader or fuhrer who would embody the national will.*

C. THE NAZI TOTALITARIAN STATE

1. Hitler ruthlessly transformed Germany into a totalitarian state. A series of laws banned all political parties except the Nazis. A special secret police called the Gestapo used sweeping powers to arbitrarily arrest anyone who opposed Nazi rule.

2. The government supervised both labor and business. New laws banned strikes and dissolved independent labor unions.

3. A ministry of culture supervised the media and shaped public opinion. Special films such as *Triumph of the Will* glorified Hitler's leadership.

4. It is interesting to note that the Nazi party's ideal German woman was a mother, wife, and homemaker.

D. ANTI-SEMITISM

1. Although Jews comprised less than 1 percent of Germany's population, Hitler blamed them for Germany's problems.

2. In 1933, the Nazis passed laws forbidding Jews to hold public office. Two years later, the Nuremberg Laws deprived Jews of German citizenship and required them to wear a yellow Star of David as identification.

3. Nazi violence against Jews steadily mounted. On November 9 and 10, 1938, the Nazis organized a "spontaneous" campaign of mob violence known as the *Kristallnacht* or Crystal Night.

VI. THE MARCH OF FASCIST AGGRESSION

A. HITLER AND THE VERSAILLES TREATY

1. In 1933, Germany withdrew from the League of Nations.
2. In 1935, Hitler openly began a program of rearmament.
3. In March 1936, Hitler ordered the German army to march into the demilitarized zone of the Rhineland.

B. MUSSOLINI AND ETHIOPIA

1. In October 1935, Mussolini ordered a massive invasion of Ethiopia.
2. The invasion represented a crucial test of the League of Nations' system of collective security.
3. Although the League condemned Italy, its members did nothing. The British and French hoped that appeasing Mussolini would maintain the peace.

C. REASONS WHY THE DEMOCRACIES FAILED TO ACT

1. The Great Depression forced the United States, Great Britain, and France to focus on domestic issues.
2. The horrific loss of life in World War I created a deep desire for peace.
3. American isolationists believed that U.S. involvement in World War I had been a mistake. They wanted to avoid becoming entangled in European affairs.
4. The democracies repeatedly underestimated Hitler's thirst for power and conquest.

D. THE SPANISH CIVIL WAR

1. Spain was a deeply divided country. Between 1931 and 1936, a democratically elected government tried to cope with the Great Depression. Led by General Francisco Franco, army leaders supported by the clergy and aristocracy favored a fascist-style government.

2. The Spanish Civil War began in 1936 when Nationalist forces led by Franco rebelled against the Republic.

3. The civil war escalated into an international ideological war when Hitler and Mussolini sent men and materials to support the Nationalists. The Russians countered by supporting the Republican, or Loyalist, side.

4. During the war, a squadron of German planes bombed the defenseless village of Guernica, killing hundreds of men, women, and children. Pablo Picasso painted *Guernica* to protest this atrocity.

5. Republican resistance finally collapsed in 1939. Franco then established an authoritarian regime that remained in power until his death in 1975. It is important to note that Spain was officially neutral during World War II.

E. THE MUNICH CONFERENCE

1. In 1938, Hitler successfully annexed Austria into Germany.

2. Hitler's campaign of German expansion focused next on a mountainous region of western Czechoslovakia called the Sudetenland. This heavily-fortified strategic region contained 3 million German-speaking people.

3. Hitler, British Prime Minister Neville Chamberlain, Mussolini, and French Premier Édouard Daladier held an emergency conference in Munich to negotiate Hitler's demand that Czechoslovakia give up the Sudetenland.

4. Chamberlain believed he could preserve the peace by appeasing Hitler and giving in to his demands.

5. The Munich Conference marked a turning point in European history. Filled with confidence, Hitler now made plans to attack Poland.

6. The Munich Conference quickly became a symbol of surrender. Following World War II, democratic leaders vowed they would never again appease a ruthless dictator.

 VII. WORLD WAR II

A. THE OUTBREAK OF WORLD WAR II

1. In August 1939, Germany and the Soviet Union stunned the world by announcing a 10-year nonaggression pact. In addition, they secretly agreed to divide eastern Europe.
2. On September 1, 1939, German forces attacked Poland. Two days later, Great Britain and France declared war on Germany.
3. Germany's blitzkrieg or "lightning war" combined fast-moving armor and air power to overwhelm Poland.

B. THE HOLOCAUST

1. The Nazi nightmare did not stop on the battlefields of Europe. Hitler ordered the systematic killing of Jews and other allegedly inferior peoples. This horrible destruction of life is known as the Holocaust.
2. The following factors contributed to the Holocaust:
   ▶ *Jews were a small and vulnerable minority.*
   ▶ *Hitler's propaganda convinced German's that Jews were an inferior race that should be eliminated.*
   ▶ *Hitler's secret police successfully stifled dissent.*
   ▶ *The Nazis successfully secured collaborators in occupied territories.*

World War II has generated fewer AP questions than any other major historic event. Although our section on World War II is very brief, it covers the topics that have generated questions. Study the Nazi-Soviet Pact, the blitzkrieg, and the Holocaust, and ignore battles and generals.

The Cold War and Beyond

I. CONTAINMENT

A. KEY POINTS

1. The Soviet Union dominated much of Eastern Europe in the aftermath of World War II. Winston Churchill warned that "an iron curtain has descended across the continent."
2. Containment was a foreign policy designed to contain or block Soviet expansion.
3. Containment was the primary U.S. foreign policy from the announcement of the Truman Doctrine in 1947 to the fall of the Berlin Wall in 1989.

B. THE TRUMAN DOCTRINE

1. The immediate goal of the Truman Doctrine was to block the expansion of Soviet influence into Greece and Turkey.
2. On March 12, 1947, President Harry Truman asked Congress for $400 million in economic aid for Greece and Turkey.
3. Truman justified the aid by declaring that the United States would support "free peoples who are resisting attempted subjugations by armed minorities or by outside pressures." This sweeping pledge became known as the Truman Doctrine.

C. THE MARSHALL PLAN

1. World War II left Western Europe devastated and vulnerable to Soviet influence.

2. The Marshall Plan was a program of economic aid designed to promote the recovery of war-torn Europe while also preventing the spread of Soviet influence.
3. The Marshall Plan was an integral part of Truman's policy of containment.
4. The Marshall Plan dramatically increased American political and economic influence in Western and Southern Europe.

D. THE NATO ALLIANCE

1. Ten Western European nations joined with the United States and Canada to form a defensive military alliance called the North Atlantic Treaty Organization (NATO). NATO coordinated defense preparations among the nations of Western Europe.
2. The NATO alliance marked a decisive break from America's tradition of isolationism.

E. THE WARSAW PACT

1. The Soviet Union responded to NATO by forming the Warsaw Pact.
2. The alliance linked the Soviet Union with seven Eastern European countries: Poland, East Germany, Czechoslovakia, Hungary, Romania, Bulgaria, and Albania.

F. THE BERLIN AIRLIFT

1. The Allies failed to agree on a peace treaty with Germany.
2. In 1945, the Allies divided Germany into four occupation zones, one each for the United States, Great Britain, France, and the Soviet Union. The city of Berlin lay 110 miles inside the Soviet occupation zone. Like Germany, it was divided into four occupation zones.
3. Fearing a resurgent Germany, the Soviet Union cut off Western land access to West Berlin. This action provoked the first great Cold War test of wills between the United States and the Soviet Union.
4. President Truman ordered a massive airlift of food, fuel, and other supplies to the beleaguered citizens of West Berlin.

5. The Berlin Airlift marked a crucial and successful test of containment.

6. Following the Berlin Airlift, the United States, Great Britain, and France created the Federal Republic of Germany or West Germany. The Soviet Union responded by establishing the East German state, the German Democratic Republic.

II. THE REVIVAL OF WESTERN EUROPE

A. ECONOMIC INTEGRATION

1. The European Coal and Steel Community
   - ▸ *Jean Monnet, a French economic planner, convinced French Premier Robert Schuman that economic cooperation would be the key to future prosperity between France and West Germany.*
   - ▸ *The Schuman Plan, as the project became known, led to the creation of the European Coal and Steel Community (ECSC).*
   - ▸ *The ECSC called for tariff-free trade in coal and steel among France, West Germany, Belgium, Italy, Luxembourg, and the Netherlands.*

2. The European Economic Community (Common Market)
   - ▸ *The ECSC proved to be a success. As a result, in 1957 its six member nations signed the Treaty of Rome creating the European Economic Community (EEC), popularly known as the Common Market.*
   - ▸ *The EEC eliminated trade barriers among its members, thus closely resembling a tariff union.*
   - ▸ *The EEC rapidly emerged as the driving force behind economic integration in Western Europe.*

APEURO test writers have focused a number of multiple-choice questions on the creation and purpose of the European Economic Community. Although the EEC is popularly known as the Common Market, test writers prefer to use its formal name. Do not confuse the Treaty of Rome with the Treaty of Maastricht. The Treaty of Rome created the EEC. The Treaty of Maastricht transformed the EEC into the European Union.

B. THE CHRISTIAN DEMOCRATS

1. Christian Democratic parties endorsed economic growth, European integration, national health insurance, aid to farmers, and political democracy.
2. Key Christian Democrat leaders included Konrad Adenauer in West Germany, Alcide de Gasperi in Italy, and Robert Schuman in France.
3. The Christian Democrats accepted Keynesian economic theory. According to Keynesian economics, governments should play a leading role in stimulating economic growth.

C. CHARLES DE GAULLE (1890–1970)

1. General Charles de Gaulle established the Fifth French Republic in 1958. He served as president until 1969.
2. De Gaulle's key foreign policy decisions included:
   ▸ *Granting Algeria full independence*
   ▸ *Withdrawing French military forces from NATO*
   ▸ *Developing France's own nuclear weapons*
   ▸ *Opposing Great Britain's entry into the EEC*

III. THE SOVIET UNION UNDER KHRUSHCHEV, 1956–1964

A. STALIN'S LAST YEARS

1. Following World War II, Joseph Stalin imposed new Five-Year Plans emphasizing extensive industrialization.
2. Stalin insisted on absolute obedience. Dissent brought imprisonment, slave labor, or death.
3. Stalin's reign of terror came to an abrupt end with his death in 1953. After a brief period of "collective leadership," Nikita Khrushchev emerged as the Soviet Union's unrivaled leader.

B. KHRUSHCHEV'S SECRET SPEECH

1. In 1956, Khrushchev boldly attacked Stalin in a "secret speech" delivered at the Twentieth Communist Party Congress in Moscow.

2. Khrushchev denounced Stalin's reign of terror and repudiated his "cult of personality."

C. DE-STALINIZATION

1. Khrushchev's program of de-Stalinization involved all of the following:
   ▸ *Shifting some resources toward producing more consumer goods*
   ▸ *Curbing the power of the secret police*
   ▸ *Granting more freedom to writers and intellectuals*
2. De-Stalinization permitted Aleksandr Solzhenitsyn to publish *One Day in the Life of Ivan Denisovich*. This short but powerful novel described the horrors of life in a Stalinist concentration camp.
3. Boris Pasternak's novel *Doctor Zhivago* illustrated the limits of de-Stalinization. The novel celebrated the human spirit and challenged the principles of communism. Although it was published in the West, Soviet censors denounced Pasternak and refused to allow him to receive the Nobel Prize for Literature.

D. SPUTNIK

1. In 1957, a beaming Khrushchev proudly announced that the Soviet Union had successfully launched a 184-pound satellite named Sputnik into orbit around the earth.
2. Sputnik quickly became a symbol of Soviet technological prowess. Sputnik's success played a key role in contributing to the space race between the Soviet Union and the United States.

E. COLD WAR CONFRONTATIONS

1. The Berlin Wall
   ▸ *Between 1949 and 1961, more than 3 million East Germans fled to West Germany by crossing into West Berlin.*
   ▸ *On August 13, 1961, the East Germans, with Khrushchev's support, began construction of a concrete wall along the border between East and West Berlin.*

▸ *The Berlin Wall stopped the flow of refugees while at the same time becoming a symbol of Communist oppression.*

2. The Cuban Missile Crisis

▸ *Khrushchev precipitated the Cuban Missile Crisis by constructing nuclear missiles in Cuba.*

▸ *After a tense confrontation with the United States, Khrushchev agreed to withdraw the missiles in exchange for a U.S. promise not to attack Fidel Castro.*

▸ *The Cuban Missile Crisis undermined Khrushchev's credibility and played a key role in his ouster from power in 1964.*

F. EASTERN EUROPE

1. De-Stalinization raised hopes for more freedom in Eastern Europe. A wave of strikes and protests swept across East Germany, Czechoslovakia, Poland, and Hungary.

2. The protests in Hungary quickly escalated into a major crisis when Hungary's liberal Communist leader, Imre Nagy, promised free elections and called for the removal of Soviet troops.

3. Khrushchev responded by ordering the Red Army to invade Hungary. After intense fighting, the Soviets crushed the rebellion and executed Nagy.

4. The United States did not assist Hungary because it lay within the Soviet sphere of influence.

Test Tip

Nikita Khrushchev has generated more APEURO multiple-choice questions than any other Russian leader except Peter the Great. Most of the questions focus on Khrushchev's secret speech and his program of de-Stalinization. While the Berlin Wall has yet to generate a released multiple-choice question, its construction and consequences have played a role in a number of free-response questions.

IV. THE SOVIET UNION UNDER BREZHNEV, 1964–1982

A. STAGNATION

1. Conservative leaders believed that Khrushchev's program of de-Stalinization posed a threat to the Communist Party's dictatorial powers.
2. Now led by Leonid Brezhnev, the Communist Party clamped down on Aleksandr Solzhenitsyn, Andrei Sakharov, and other outspoken dissidents.
3. Brezhnev's hard-line policies led to a prolonged period of political repression and economic stagnation.

B. CZECHOSLOVAKIA AND THE BREZHNEV DOCTRINE

1. In Czechoslovakia, a new communist leader, Alexander Dubček, initiated a program of democratic reforms saying he wanted to create "socialism with a human face."
2. Alarmed by Dubček's reforms, Brezhnev called on the other Warsaw Pact countries to invade Czechoslovakia and remove Dubček from power.
3. Brezhnev justified the invasion by claiming that the Soviet Union and its allies had the right to intervene in the domestic affairs of other Communist countries. This declaration became known as the Brezhnev Doctrine.
4. The United States refrained from taking any action because Czechoslovakia lay within the Soviet sphere of influence.

C. DÉTENTE

1. President Richard Nixon initiated a policy of détente to reduce tensions with the Soviet Union. The two superpowers agreed to limit nuclear arms and expand trade.
2. The Helsinki Accords marked the high point of Cold War détente. The accords ratified the European territorial boundaries established after World War II and committed the signers to recognize and protect basic human rights.

CHRONOLOGICAL REVIEW

V. **THE COLLAPSE OF EUROPEAN COMMUNISM**

A. GORBACHEV'S REFORMS

1. In March 1985, members of the Politburo, the Communist Party's top decision-making group, selected Mikhail Gorbachev as the new leader of the Soviet Union.

2. When Gorbachev took power, the Soviet Union was still the world's most feared totalitarian dictatorship. But Gorbachev recognized that "something was wrong." Blaming poor living conditions on the country's rigid political system and stagnant economy, he launched an unprecedented program of reforms.

3. Glasnost
   ▶ *Soviet leaders from Vladimir Lenin to Brezhnev created a totalitarian state that controlled the mass media and restricted human rights.*
   ▶ *In 1986, Gorbachev introduced a new policy known as glasnost, or openness, which encouraged Soviet citizens to discuss ways to reform their society.*

4. Perestroika
   ▶ *Glasnost gave Soviet citizens an opportunity to complain publicly about their economic problems.*
   ▶ *In 1986, Gorbachev launched a program called perestroika, or economic restructuring, to revitalize the Soviet economy.*

5. *Demokratizatsiya*
   ▶ *Gorbachev understood that in order for the economy to thrive, the Communist Party would have to loosen its grip on Soviet society.*
   ▶ *In 1989, Gorbachev unveiled a third new policy called demokratizatsiya, or democratization. The plan called for the election of a new legislature, the 2,250-member Congress of People's Deputies.*

B. MAKING COMPARISONS: STALIN AND GORBACHEV

1. Stalin
   ▶ *Rejected the relatively free markets created by Lenin's New Economic Policy*

> ▸ *Implemented a series of Five-Year Plans that promoted state planning and industrialization*
> ▸ *Forced peasant farmers to work on huge state-run and state-owned farms called collectives*
> ▸ *Purged party leaders who showed the slightest degree of dissent from his policies*
> ▸ *Imprisoned and executed millions of Soviet citizens*
> ▸ *Created a rigid totalitarian state*
> ▸ *Imposed Soviet control over Eastern Europe*

2. Gorbachev

> ▸ *Advocated private ownership of property and free markets*
> ▸ *Allowed public discussion and criticism of Communist Party policies*
> ▸ *Permitted openly contested elections*
> ▸ *Allowed national minorities within the Soviet Union to express pent-up grievances*
> ▸ *Encouraged East Europeans to reform their political systems without fear of Soviet armed intervention*
> ▸ *Raised expectations in the Soviet Union and Eastern Europe for greater freedom*

C. POLAND AND SOLIDARITY

1. The people of Poland were the first to test Gorbachev's new policies.
2. Led by Lech Walesa, Polish workers formed a democratic trade union called Solidarity.
3. Pope John Paul II provided crucial support for the Solidarity labor movement in Poland.
4. In 1989, Polish voters overwhelmingly rejected the Communist Party and elected Solidarity candidates. This marked the first time the people of a nation peacefully turned a Communist regime out of power.

D. THE FALL OF THE BERLIN WALL

1. Inspired by the events in Poland, the people of East Germany demanded change in their government.

2. On November 9, 1989, a new East German leader opened the Berlin Wall. The reunification of Germany occurred less than one year later. These watershed events marked the end of the Cold War in Eastern Europe.

E. THE COLLAPSE OF THE SOVIET UNION

1. The collapse of the Communist regimes in Eastern Europe inspired ethnic groups within the Soviet Union.
2. Gorbachev's policy of glasnost loosened controls, enabling ethnic protests to spread across the Soviet Union.
3. In a last desperate effort to preserve the Soviet Union, Communist hard-liners attempted to overthrow Gorbachev with a military coup.
4. The hard-liners assumed that a show of force would ensure obedience. They were wrong. Under Gorbachev's reforms, people had lost their fear of the party and were willing to defend their freedom.
5. Led by Boris Yeltsin, president of the Russian Republic, the Russian people thwarted the coup.
6. On December 25, 1991, Gorbachev announced his resignation as president of a country that by then had ceased to exist. One former colleague observed sadly, "He tried to reform the unreformable."

VI. KEY SOCIAL AND DEMOGRAPHIC TRENDS

A. KEY DEMOGRAPHIC TRENDS

1. European birth rates rose in the 1950s but then began a sustained decline.
2. As a result of decolonization, former colonial peoples migrated to Europe.
3. Immigration from North Africa and the Middle East created significant Muslim populations in many Western European countries.
4. Attracted by economic opportunities, southern Europeans migrated to northern Europe.

B. KEY CHANGES IN WOMEN'S RIGHTS AND ROLES

1. Led by Simone de Beauvoir, European feminists called attention to social problems that women faced and also emphasized the need for women to control their own lives.
2. Major feminist goals included the following:
    ▶ *Expanded employment opportunities*
    ▶ *Expanded child-care facilities*
    ▶ *Improved access to birth control information*
    ▶ *Liberalized divorce laws*
3. During the postwar period, European women married earlier and had fewer children.
4. Employment rates for married women dramatically increased.

PART III:

KEY THEMES
and Facts

Key Figures in European Intellectual History

NICCOLÒ MACHIAVELLI (1469–1527)

1. Renaissance political philosopher who wrote *The Prince*
2. Believed that people are ungrateful and untrustworthy
3. Urged rulers to study war, avoid unnecessary kindness, and always base policy upon the principle that the end justifies the means

DESIDERIUS ERASMUS (1466–1536)

1. Northern humanist who wrote *In Praise of Folly*
2. Wrote in Latin while most humanists wrote in the vernacular
3. Wanted to reform the Catholic Church, not destroy it

MARTIN LUTHER (1483–1546)

1. Protestant reformer whose criticism of indulgences helped spark the Reformation
2. Advocated salvation by faith, the authority of the Bible, and a priesthood of all believers
3. Believed that Christian women should strive to become models of wifely obedience and Christian charity

JOHN CALVIN (1509–1564)

1. Protestant reformer who wrote *The Institutes of the Christian Religion*
2. Believed in the absolute omnipotence of God, the weakness of humanity, and the doctrine of predestination
3. Established Geneva as a model Christian community

4. Influenced followers who were known as Huguenots in France, Presbyterians in Scotland, and Puritans in England and the New England colonies

5. Advocated that each local congregation have a ruling body composed of both ministers and laymen who carefully supervised the moral conduct of the faithful

It is important to understand the similarities and differences between Luther and Calvin. Both were Protestant reformers who challenged the pope and relied upon the Bible as the sole source of religious authority. Unlike Luther, Calvin formulated a systematic theology that stressed predestination. In addition, while Luther relied on state churches, Calvin devised a flexible system of church government that resisted control by the state.

MICHEL DE MONTAIGNE (1533–1592)

1. French Renaissance writer who developed the essay as a literary genre

2. Known for his skeptical attitude and willingness to look at all sides of an issue

NICOLAUS COPERNICUS (1473–1543)

1. Polish clergyman and astronomer who wrote *On the Revolution of the Heavenly Spheres*

2. Helped launch the Scientific Revolution by challenging the widespread belief in the geocentric theory that the earth is the center of the universe

3. Offered a new heliocentric universe in which the earth and the other planets revolve around the sun

JOHANNES KEPLER (1571–1630)

1. Began his career as an assistant to the Danish astronomer Tycho Brahe

2. Formulated three laws of planetary motion

3. Proved that planetary orbits are elliptical rather than circular

GALILEO GALILEI (1564–1642)

1. Italian scientist who contributed to the scientific method by conducting controlled experiments
2. Major accomplishments included using the telescope for astronomical observation, formulating laws of motion, and popularizing the new scientific ideas
3. Condemned by the Inquisition for publicly advocating Copernicus's heliocentric theory

ISSAC NEWTON (1642–1727)

1. English scientist and mathematician who wrote the *Principia*
2. Viewed the universe as a vast machine governed by the universal laws of gravity and inertia
3. Mechanistic view of the universe strongly influenced deism

FRANCIS BACON (1561–1626)

1. English politician and writer
2. Formalized the empirical method into a general theory of inductive reasoning known as empiricism

RENÉ DESCARTES (1596–1650)

1. French philosopher and mathematician
2. Used deductive reasoning from self-evident principles to reach scientific laws

Don't confuse Bacon and Descartes. Both contributed to seventeenth-century scientific development by articulating theories of the scientific method. Remember that Bacon's inductive method is based upon observation while Descartes's deductive method is based upon systematic doubt and the use of mathematics to express scientific laws.

THOMAS HOBBES (1588–1679)

1. English political philosopher who wrote *Leviathan*
2. Viewed human beings as naturally self-centered and prone to violence
3. Feared the dangers of anarchy more than the dangers of tyranny
4. Argued that monarchs have absolute and unlimited political authority

JOHN LOCKE (1632–1704)

1. English philosopher who wrote *The Second Treatise of Government*
2. Viewed humans as basically rational beings who learn from experience
3. Formulated the theory of natural rights, arguing that people are born with basic rights to "life, liberty, and property"
4. Insisted that governments are formed to protect natural rights
5. Stated that the governed have a right to rebel against rulers who violate natural rights

VOLTAIRE (1694–1778)

1. French philosophe and voluminous author of essays and letters
2. Championed the enlightened principles of reason, progress, toleration, and individual liberty
3. Opposed superstition, intolerance, and ignorance
4. Criticized organized religion for perpetuating superstition and intolerance

JEAN-JACQUES ROUSSEAU (1712–1778)

1. Enlightened thinker best known for writing *The Social Contract* and *Emile*
2. Believed that since "law is the expression of the general will," the state is based on a social contract

3. Emphasized the education of the whole person for citizenship

4. Rejected excessive rationalism and stressed emotions, thus anticipating the romantic movement

ADAM SMITH (1723–1790)

1. Scottish economist who wrote *An Inquiry into the Nature and Causes of the Wealth of Nations*

2. Opposed mercantilist policies

3. Advocated free trade and "the Invisible Hand of competition"

MARY WOLLSTONECRAFT (1759–1797)

1. British writer, philosopher, and feminist who wrote *A Vindication of the Rights of Woman*

2. Argued that women are not naturally inferior to men

3. Maintained that women deserve the same fundamental rights as men

EDMUND BURKE (1729–1797)

1. English conservative leader who wrote *Reflections on the Revolution in France*

2. Denounced the radicalism and violence of the French Revolution

3. Favored gradual and orderly change

JOHN STUART MILL (1806–1873)

1. English Utilitarian and essayist best known for writing *On Liberty* and *The Subjection of Women*

2. Advocated women's rights and endorsed universal suffrage

KARL MARX (1818–1883)

1. Scientific socialist who coauthored *The Communist Manifesto*

2. Believed that the history of class conflict is best understood through the dialectical process of thesis, antithesis, and synthesis

KEY THEMES AND FACTS

3. Contended that a class struggle between the bourgeoisie and the proletariat would lead "to the dictatorship of the proletariat," which in turn would be a transitional phase leading to a classless society

CHARLES DARWIN (1809–1882)

1. British biologist who wrote *The Origin of Species*
2. Challenged the idea of special creation by proposing a revolutionary theory of biological evolution
3. Concluded that every living plant and animal takes part in a constant "struggle for existence" in which only the "fittest" survive
4. Argued that the fittest are determined by a process of natural selection

SIGMUND FREUD (1856–1939)

1. Austrian psychologist who formulated groundbreaking theories of human personality
2. Theorized that the human psyche contains three distinct parts: (1) the id, which is the center of unconscious sexual and aggressive drives; (2) the superego, which is the center of moral values; and (3) the ego, which is the center of pragmatic reason
3. Argued that human behavior is often irrational

ALBERT EINSTEIN (1879–1955)

1. German physicist whose theory of special relativity undermined Newtonian physics
2. Challenged traditional conceptions of time, space, and motion
3. Contributed to the view that humans live in a universe with uncertainties
4. Added to the feeling of uncertainty in the postwar world

FRIEDRICH NIETZCHE (1844–1900)

1. German philosopher whose writings influenced existentialism
2. Expressed contempt for middle-class morality, saying that it led to a false and shallow existence
3. Rejected reason and embraced the irrational
4. Believed that the "will-to-power" of a few heroic "supermen" could successfully reorder the world

ALBERT CAMUS (1913–1960) AND JEAN-PAUL SARTRE (1905–1980)

1. French existentialist philosophers and writers
2. Questioned the efficacy of reason and science to understand the human situation
3. Believed that God, reason, and progress are myths, and that humans live in a hostile world, alone and isolated

Key Events in European Diplomatic History

THE PEACE OF AUGSBURG, 1555

1. Ended the religious civil war between Roman Catholics and Lutherans in the German states
2. Gave each German prince the right to determine the religion of his state, either Roman Catholic or Lutheran
3. Failed to provide for the recognition of Calvinists or other religious groups

THE COUNCIL OF TRENT, 1545–1563

1. Reformed Catholic Church discipline and reaffirmed church doctrine
2. Preserved the papacy as the center of Christianity
3. Confirmed all seven existing sacraments
4. Reaffirmed Latin as the language of worship
5. Forbade clerical marriage

THE EDICT OF NANTES, 1598

1. Issued by Henry IV of France
2. Granted religious toleration to French Protestants
3. Marked the first formal recognition by a European national monarchy that two religions could coexist in the same country
4. Revoked by Louis XIV in 1685

THE PEACE OF WESTPHALIA, 1648

1. Ended the Thirty Years' War
2. Recognized Calvinism as a legally permissible faith
3. Recognized the sovereign independent authority of over 300 German states
4. Continued the political fragmentation of Germany
5. Granted Sweden additional territory, confirming its status as a major power
6. Acknowledged the independence of the United Provinces of the Netherlands

THE PEACE OF UTRECHT, 1713

1. Ended Louis XIV's efforts to dominate Europe
2. Allowed Philip V to remain on the throne of Spain but stipulated that the crowns of Spain and France should never be worn by the same monarch
3. Granted the Spanish Netherlands (now called the Austrian Netherlands) to the Austrian Habsburgs along with Milan, Naples, and Sicily
4. Granted England a number of territories including Newfoundland, Nova Scotia, and Gibraltar
5. Granted England the asiento, the lucrative right to supply African slaves to Spanish America

THE PRAGMATIC SANCTION, 1713

1. Guaranteed the succession of Habsburg emperor Charles VI's eldest daughter, Maria Theresa, to the throne
2. Guaranteed the indivisibility of the Habsburg lands
3. Violated when Frederick the Great of Prussia invaded Silesia in 1740

THE CONGRESS OF VIENNA, 1815

1. Enacted a settlement that was acceptable to both the victors and to France
2. Created a balance of power that lasted until the unification of Germany in 1871

3. Underestimated the forces of liberalism and nationalism

4. Used the principle of legitimacy to restore the Bourbons to the French throne

5. United Belgium with the Netherlands to form a single kingdom of the Netherlands

6. Created a loose confederation of 39 German states dominated by Austria

THE BERLIN CONFERENCE, 1884–1885

1. Established rules for dividing Africa amongst the European powers. A European state could no longer simply declare a region of Africa its colony. It first had to exercise effective control over the territory.

2. Declared the Congo to be the "Congo Free State," under the personal control of Leopold II of Belgium.

3. Established rules governing the race for African colonies

THE TREATY OF VERSAILLES, 1919

1. Refused to allow either defeated Germany or Communist Russia to participate in peace conference negotiations

2. Forced Germany to sign a war-guilt clause that was used to justify imposing large war reparations payments

3. Changed the map of Europe by returning Alsace-Lorraine to France and dissolving Austria-Hungary into the separate states of Austria, Hungary, Czechoslovakia, and Yugoslavia

4. Created the League of Nations to discuss and settle disputes without resorting to war

5. Left a legacy of bitterness between the victors and Germany

Test Tip

The Congress of Vienna and the Treaty of Versailles have generated a significant number of multiple-choice and free-response questions. Released APEURO tests contain almost 20 multiple-choice questions on these two topics. In addition, test writers have frequently asked students to compare and contrast the achievements and failures of the Congress of Vienna and the Versailles Treaty. Needless to say, it is vital that you carefully study these two key conferences in European diplomatic history.

THE TREATY OF BREST-LITOVSK, 1918

1. Ended Bolshevik Russia's participation in World War I
2. Negotiated by Vladimir Lenin because he was unwilling to risk Bolshevik gains by continuing a war that could no longer be won
3. Nullified following Germany's defeat by the Allies

THE LOCARNO PACT, 1925

1. Recorded an agreement between France and Germany to respect mutual frontiers
2. Marked the beginning of a brief period of reduced tensions among the European powers

THE KELLOGG-BRIAND PACT, 1928

1. Outlawed war as an instrument of national policy
2. Violated repeatedly during the 1930s

THE MUNICH CONFERENCE, 1938

1. Ceded the Sudetenland to Adolf Hitler
2. Discredited the British policy of appeasement

THE NAZI-SOVIET NONAGGRESSION PACT, 1939

1. Created a nonaggression agreement in which Hitler and Joseph Stalin promised to remain neutral if the other became involved in a war
2. Divided eastern Europe into German and Soviet zones

NORTH ATLANTIC PACT, 1949

1. Established the North Atlantic Treaty Organization (NATO) to coordinate the defense of its members
2. Implemented Harry Truman's policy of containing the Soviet Union

3. Forced to move its headquarters from Paris to Brussels when Charles de Gaulle withdrew French forces from the "American-controlled" NATO

THE TREATY OF ROME, 1957

1. Created the European Economic Community (EEC), generally known as the Common Market
2. Marked the beginning of European economic integration

THE HELSINKI ACCORDS, 1975

1. Ratified the European territorial boundaries established after World War II
2. Established "Helsinki watch committees" to monitor human rights in the 35 nations that signed the Helsinki Accords
3. Marked the high point of Cold War détente

THE MAASTRICHT TREATY, 1991

1. Created the European Union (EU), the world's largest single economic market
2. Created a central bank for the European Union

Test Tip

It is easy to neglect the Maastricht Treaty since it occurs near the end of your APEURO course. In fact, because of time constraints many students and teachers fail to reach this topic. Don't make the mistake of forgetting to study this treaty. It is frequently tested and often appears as one of the last questions in the multiple-choice section.

Key Events, Trends, and Figures in European Women's History

THE RENAISSANCE

1. In *The Courtier*, Baldassare Castiglione wrote that the perfect court lady should be well educated and charming. Women, however, were not expected to seek fame as men did.

2. Christine de Pizan was a prolific author who wrote a history of famous women and is now remembered as Europe's first feminist.

3. Isabella d'Este was the most famous Renaissance woman. Her life illustrates that being a patron of the arts was the most socially acceptable role for a well-educated Renaissance woman.

THE REFORMATION

1. Martin Luther believed that Christian women should strive to be models of obedience and Christian charity.

2. The Protestant Reformation reduced access to convents, thus changing the role of sixteenth-century women.

3. Quakers regularly allowed women to preach.

4. Older, widowed women were most often accused of practicing witchcraft.

THE ENLIGHTENMENT

1. Women played a leading role in hosting salons. Salons gave educated women a voice in cultural affairs. Madame Geoffrin was the most influential of the salon hostesses.

2. Support for superstition and witchcraft declined as educated Europeans turned to rational explanations for natural events.

THE EIGHTEENTH CENTURY

1. Most young married European couples lived in nuclear families. Large multigenerational households were not the norm.

2. Most couples postponed marriage until they were in their mid- to late 20s.

3. Young peasant women increasingly left home to work as domestic servants.

THE FRENCH REVOLUTION

1. Women led the march to Versailles to demand cheap bread and to force the royal family to move to Paris.

2. Women did not gain the right to vote or to hold political office.

3. Olympia de Gouges wrote the *Declaration of the Rights of Woman and of the Female Citizen*. She demanded that French women be given the same rights as men.

4. Mary Wollstonecraft wrote *A Vindication of the Rights of Women*. She argued that women are not naturally inferior to men. They only appear to be inferior because of a lack of education.

5. Napoleon Bonaparte's Civil Code reasserted the Old Regime's patriarchal system. The Code granted husbands extensive control over their wives. For example, married women needed their husband's consent to dispose of their own property. Divorce and property rights taken away by the Napoleonic Code were not fully restored until 1881.

THE NINETEENTH CENTURY

1. John Stuart Mill wrote *The Subjection of Women*. He argued that the social and legal inequalities imposed on women were a relic from the past.

2. Henrik Ibsen's *A Doll's House* criticized conventional marriage roles.

3. The ideal middle-class woman was expected to be an "angel in the house." Her most important roles were to be a devoted mother and the family's moral guardian.

4. Rising standards of living made it possible for men and women to marry at a younger age. At the same time, the rising cost of child rearing caused a decline in the size of middle-class families.

5. Few married women worked outside the home. Most working women were single.

6. Opportunities for well-educated women were limited to teaching, nursing, and social work.

7. Law codes in most European countries gave women few legal rights. Divorce was legalized in Britain in 1857 and in France in 1884. However, Catholic countries such as Spain and Italy did not permit divorce.

8. Nineteenth-century women's rights advocates worked for the right of women to control their own property.

9. By the end of the nineteenth century, educated middle-class "new women" enjoyed more independent lifestyles.

10. As mass culture developed, fashion magazines made middle-class and working-class women more aware of style. At the same time, booksellers began to publish more fictional romances as well as articles and poems by female authors.

WOMEN'S SUFFRAGE

1. Although the women's suffrage movement commanded wide attention, it achieved few successes. In 1900, no country in Europe allowed women the right to vote.

2. Led by Emmeline Pankhurst, British women waged an aggressive campaign for women's suffrage.

3. During World War I, millions of women replaced men in factories, offices, and shops.

4. In 1918, Parliament granted the suffrage to women over the age of 30.

WOMEN IN THE SOVIET UNION

1. Marxists argued that both capitalism and middle-class husbands exploited women.

2. The Bolsheviks proclaimed complete equality of rights for women.

3. Soviet women were urged to work outside the home. Divorce and abortion were both easily available.

4. Soviet women were encouraged to become professionals. By 1950, women comprised three-quarters of the doctors in the Soviet Union.

WORLD WAR II

1. During the 1930s, Italy and Germany encouraged women to remain at home and provide their countries with more offspring.

2. During World War II, the commitment to total war caused millions of women to enter the workforce.

3. Women contributed directly to the war effort by serving as nurses and medics. In the Soviet Union, women known as "night witches" served as combat pilots.

4. Postwar reconstruction required women to continue working.

5. French and Italian women gained the franchise in 1945.

POST–WORLD WAR II FEMINISM

1. Led by Simone de Beauvoir, European feminists called attention to social problems that women faced. De Beauvoir also emphasized the need for women to control their own lives.

2. European feminists worked for liberalized divorce laws, improved access to birth control information, and expanded child-care facilities.

3. During the postwar period, European women married earlier and gave birth to fewer children.

4. Employment rates for married women dramatically increased.

PART IV:

TEST-TAKING STRATEGIES

Chapter 6

Strategies for the Multiple-Choice Questions

Your APEURO exam will begin with a 55-minute section containing 80 multiple-choice questions. These questions begin with the High Renaissance in 1450 and end with the dawn of the twenty-first century in 2001. In reality, the 1991 Maastricht Treaty is the most recent topic covered by the test.

Each multiple-choice question is worth 1.125 points. The 80 multiple-choice questions are thus worth a total of 90 points or half of the 180 points that are on the APEURO exam. Recently, the College Board changed the scoring of the multiple-choice sections of AP exams. The score achieved on the multiple-choice section of the exam will be based on the number of questions answered correctly. Points will not be deducted for incorrect answers or unanswered questions.

With this change, the "guessing penalty" is eliminated, but don't waste precious time. If you do not have any idea how to answer a question, skip it and move on. If you can eliminate two or more answers, you should use the process of elimination to take an educated guess.

A GRAND STRATEGY

The multiple-choice questions are vital to achieving a high score. Although they account for just under one-third of the APEURO exam's total time, they are worth 50 percent of the exam's total points. On the 2004 exam a test-taker needed only 121 points to score a 5 and 99 points to score a 4.

The multiple-choice questions cover very predictable topics. About one-fourth of the questions will be devoted to the definitions of key topics and the provisions of key treaties and agreements. Another 10 questions will cover key intellectual figures. In addition, most exams devote 8 to 12 questions to charts, political cartoons, maps, and identifying the style of famous works of art. These graphic questions are particularly straightforward, since all of the information you need is provided in the chart, cartoon, map, or picture.

Chapters 2 to 25 in this book contain all of the information you will need to ace the multiple-choice questions. If you carefully review these chapters, you should be able to correctly answer at least 60 of the 80 multiple-choice questions. If you miss 12 questions and leave 8 blank, this will give you a raw score of 64.50 points. You will then need only another 56.50 points to score a 5 and just 34.50 points to score a 4!

TWO CHALLENGING FORMATS

Most APEURO multiple-choice questions are straightforward. However, test writers do use two formats that require closer examination.

"EXCEPT" QUESTIONS

Between two and four questions on each exam will provide you with four answers that are correct and one answer choice that is incorrect. Known as EXCEPT questions, these problems ask you to find the answer that does not fit or is incorrect. The best strategy is to treat these questions as if they were five-part true-false questions. Simply go through the questions and label each answer choice "true" or "false." The correct answer is the one that is false. Here are three examples:

1. **Mercantilist theory emphasized all of the following EXCEPT**

    (A) *recognizing that the wealth of nations was limited and needed to be carefully preserved*

    (B) *using tariffs to protect domestic industries*

(C)   *securing a favorable balance of trade*

(D)   *acquiring colonies to manufacture inexpensive finished goods*

(E)   *building a strong merchant marine*

Answer choices A, B, C, and E are all true. Since only D is false, it is the correct answer. Mercantilists advocated acquiring colonies to supply raw materials and purchase manufactured goods from their "mother" country.

2.   **The regime of Louis XIV was characterized by all of the following EXCEPT**

(A)   *royal patronage of the arts*

(B)   *renewal of the Edict of Nantes*

(C)   *support for Jean-Baptiste Colbert's mercantilist policies*

(D)   *wars intended to extend French territory to its "natural frontiers"*

(E)   *the use of absolute power justified by Jacques-Bénigne Bossuet's doctrine of the divine right of kings*

Answer choices A, C, D, and E are all true. Since only B is false, it is the correct answer. Louis XIV revoked the Edict of Nantes in 1685.

3.   **Nineteenth-century liberals advocated all of the following EXCEPT**

(A)   *the sanctity of private property*

(B)   *laissez-faire economics*

(C)   *the abolition of slavery*

(D)   *constitutional government*

(E)   *universal suffrage for men and women*

Answer choices A, B, C, and D are all true. Since only E is false, it is the correct answer. Nineteenth-century liberals did not advocate universal suffrage for men and women. In fact, in 1900 no European country granted women the right to vote.

QUOTE QUESTIONS

Between four and six questions on each exam will provide you with a quote and ask you to link the quote to a key person, term, or document. Many of the quotes are well known, while others are not. Regardless of whether the quote is famous or obscure, it will have a key word, phrase, or definition that will clearly establish its purpose. Your job is to find the key parts of the quote and connect them to the answer. Here are three examples:

1. **"It is necessary for him who lays out a state and arranges laws for it to presuppose that all men are evil and that they are always going to act according to the wickedness of their spirits whenever they have free scope."**

   The political advice above can be found in

   (A) *Martin Luther's* Ninety-five Theses

   (B) *Desiderius Erasmus's* The Praise of Folly

   (C) *Niccolò Machiavelli's* The Prince

   (D) *Adam Smith's* The Wealth of Nations

   (E) *Charles Darwin's* The Origin of Species

   The key phrase in this quote states, "It is necessary for him who lays out a state and arranges laws for it to presuppose that all men are evil ..." You should therefore look for a political writer who assumed that humans are "evil." Choice A can be eliminated since Luther's *Ninety-five Theses* was concerned with the abuse of indulgences. Choice B can be eliminated since Erasmus's *The Praise of Folly* was a satire poking fun at human nature. Choice D can be eliminated since Adam Smith's *The Wealth of Nations* was concerned with discussing economic principles. While Smith would have described humans as motivated by self-interest, he would not have said that "all men are evil." Choice E can be eliminated because Darwin's *The Origin of Species* was concerned with establishing the principles of evolution. Only Choice C is correct. Machiavelli's *The Prince* is a political treatise designed to guide rulers on how to gain, maintain, and increase power. Machiavelli had a very pessimistic view of human nature.

2. **"Let us then suppose the mind to be, as we say, white paper, void of all characters, without any ideas: how comes it to be furnished? To this I answer, in one word, from EXPERIENCE. In that all our knowledge is founded; and from that it ultimately derives itself."**

    The theory described above was developed by

    (A) *John Calvin*

    (B) *Johannes Kepler*

    (C) *John Locke*

    (D) *Isaac Newton*

    (E) *Karl Marx*

    The key word in this quote is "EXPERIENCE." It literally jumps off the page and exclaims, "I'm it!" Choice A can be eliminated since Calvin was a theologian concerned with predestination. Choice B can be eliminated since Kepler was an astronomer concerned with formulating laws of planetary motion. Choice D can be eliminated since Newton was a physicist concerned with formulating the laws of gravity and inertia. Choice E can be eliminated since Marx was a scientific socialist concerned with the dialectics of class struggle. Choice C is the correct answer. John Locke clearly stated that people are basically rational and learn from practical experience.

3. **"Without openness there is not, and there cannot be, democratism, the political creativity of the masses and their participation in management."**

    The passage above most accurately describes

    (A) *Vladimir Lenin's theory of the dictatorship of the proletariat*

    (B) *Joseph Stalin's defense of his political purges*

(C) *Karl Marx's belief that a classless society will emerge at the end of the dialectical process*

(D) *Friedrich Nietzche's rejection of God and bourgeois morality*

(E) *Mikhail Gorbachev's concept of glasnost*

The key word in this quote is "openness." Openness or *glasnost* was one of the key features of Mikhail Gorbachev's attempt to reform Soviet society. Choice E is the correct answer.

Strategies for the Document-Based Essay Question

After completing the multiple-choice section, you will have a well-deserved 10-minute break. When you return to your desk, your exam will resume with the document-based essay question (DBQ). The DBQ is an essay question that requires you to interpret and analyze 11 or 12 brief primary-source documents. The documents are typically excerpts from diaries, speeches, letters, reports, and official decrees. In addition, the documents often include a graph, map, political cartoon, or work of art.

The DBQ begins with a mandatory 15-minute reading period. You should use this time to read the documents, organize your thoughts, determine a thesis, and prepare an outline for your essay. You will have 45 minutes to write your essay.

Your DBQ essay will be scored on a scale from 1 to 9. Each scale point is worth 4.5 exam points. So a perfect score of 9 is worth 40.5 points, a 6 is worth 27 points, and a 4 is worth 18 points. It is important to remember that a 6 will keep you on pace to earn an overall score of 5 on the APEURO exam.

THE DBQ SCORING SYSTEM: BASIC CORE POINTS

The APEURO DBQ scoring system begins with a set of six Basic Core points, each of which is worth one point. Here are the six Basic Core points and the skills they measure:

1. **Provides a thesis that clearly and directly addresses all parts of the question**
    - ▸ *Your thesis must address all parts of the question.*
    - ▸ *The most common mistake students make is to write a thesis that is too general or that focuses on only one part of the question.*

2. **Discusses a majority of the documents individually and specifically**
    ▸ *You must discuss at least seven documents to receive credit for this point.*
    ▸ *You must refer to each document by citing either its number, its name, or its author.*

3. **Demonstrates an understanding of the basic meaning of the documents**
    ▸ *The scoring rules state that you may misinterpret no more than one document.*
    ▸ *A misinterpretation typically occurs when you place a document in the wrong group. It can also occur when a faulty analysis leads you to an inaccurate conclusion.*

4. **Supports the thesis with appropriate interpretations of a majority of the documents.**
    ▸ *Remember, you must use at least seven of the documents.*
    ▸ *The documents must support your thesis.*

5. **Analyzes the point of view or bias in at least three documents**
    ▸ *Point-of-view analysis is extremely important. As you read each document, try to understand why the author expresses a particular point of view.*
    ▸ *Always try to understand an author's motive for expressing a point of view.*

6. **Analyzes documents by organizing them into at least three appropriate groups**
    ▸ *The documents are not a random assortment of readings. They cluster around the key parts of the DBQ assignment.*
    ▸ *A group must contain at least two documents.*
    ▸ *A document can be used in more than one group.*

THE DBQ SCORING SYSTEM: EXPANDED CORE POINTS

You must earn a basic score of 6 in order to be eligible for expanded core points. You can earn up to three additional points by demonstrating the following skills:

▶ *Having a clear, analytical, and comprehensive thesis*
▶ *Using all or almost all of the 11 to 12 documents*
▶ *Skillfully using the documents to support your thesis*
▶ *Displaying an understanding of the nuances or shades of difference among the documents*
▶ *Analyzing the point of view or bias in at least four documents*
▶ *Discussing how key ideas, institutions, and trends change over time*
▶ *Bringing in relevant outside information*

PRACTICE MATERIALS

Practice is the key to performing well on the DBQ. Although practice will not necessarily lead to a perfect score, it will help you earn a high score. College Board materials are the best source of practice DBQs. The *2009 AP European History Released Exam* and the *2004 AP European History Released Exam* both include actual DBQs and scored sample essays. Both of these booklets can be purchased from the College Board's online store. In addition, you should go to the AP European History Course homepage at AP Central (*www.apcentral.collegeboard.com*). You will find DBQs and sample essays from 1999 to the present.

STRATEGIES FOR SUCCESS

Using authentic practice materials is important. Following good strategies is essential. This section will use the DBQ from the 2008 APEURO exam to provide you with a guided set of strategies that can be used for any DBQ.

1. **Carefully analyze the assignment.**

   Begin your 15-minute mandatory reading period by carefully examining the assignment. The 2008 DBQ asked students to "analyze the causes of and responses to the peasants' revolts in the German states, 1524–1526." This assignment gives you two very specific tasks: first, analyze the causes of the peasants' revolts; second, analyze the responses to the peasants' revolts.

2. **Carefully examine each document and create an organizational chart.**

Your next step is to read, analyze, and organize the documents. The 2008 DBQ included the following 12 documents:

Document 1: A report from Leonhard von Eck to Duke Ludwig of Bavaria

Document 2: An excerpt from the *Twelve Articles of the Swabian Peasants*

Document 3: An excerpt from the *Articles of the Peasants of Memmingen*

Document 4: An excerpt from the Memmingen Town Council's reply to the *Articles of the Peasants of Memmingen*

Document 5: A pastor's report on the events at Weinsburg

Document 6: A peasant leader's open letter to the people of Allstedt

Document 7: An excerpt from Martin Luther's *Against the Murdering, Thieving Hordes of Peasants*

Document 8: A secret report to the Archbishop of Würzburg

Document 9: A town councilor's letter to Duke Albert of Prussia

Document 10: A nobleman's plea for leniency

Document 11: A noble's letter to Duke Albert of Prussia

Document 12: An excerpt from the Decree of the Imperial Diet of Speyer

Many students find it very helpful to organize the documents by placing them into a chart. Your first column should always be labeled "Point of View." Remember, you must analyze the point of view or bias of at least three documents. Your headings for the next two columns will be "Causes" and "Responses," respectively. It is very important to remember that you don't have to fill in each cell in your chart. Here is an example of what your chart could look like:

	Point of View	Causes	Responses
Document 1	High government official—wants to preserve order	Religious influences	Condemnation; unfavorable
Document 2	Peasant leader	Economic relief; oppression	Conciliatory; favorable
Document 3	Peasant parliament— widely held views	Religious influences; economic relief; oppression	Conciliatory; favorable
Document 4	Town—guided by economic self-interest		Conciliatory
Document 5	Pastor		Riots/ plundering; unfavorable
Document 6	Peasant leader	Religious influences	Riots/ plundering; favorable
Document 7	Martin Luther— dependent on princes for protection		Condemnation; unfavorable

(continued)

	Point of View	Causes	Responses
Document 8	Secret report—likely to be a candid assessment	Economic relief; oppression	Condemnation; unfavorable
Document 9	Town letter	Oppression	Conciliatory; favorable
Document 10	Nobleman's plea		Condemnation; unfavorable
Document 11	Represents the nobility		Condemnation; unfavorable
Document 12	Imperial decree		Condemnation; unfavorable

3. **Carefully determine your thesis.**

A thesis is your position on the assigned topic. It must address both the causes of and responses to the peasants' revolts. Having a clearly defined and focused thesis is absolutely essential. If you have not fully formulated your thesis during the 15-minute mandatory thinking period, do not panic. There is no rule saying that you must begin writing after the 15 minutes are up. It is better to take a few extra minutes to mentally work on your thesis than to rush and end up with a weak thesis.

Here is a sample thesis statement for the 2008 DBQ:

The German peasants' revolts of 1524–1526 were the largest popular uprisings in Europe before the French Revolution of 1789. Economic grievances justified by Protestant religious ideas combined to cause the revolts. Responses varied depending upon social class. Peasants offered moderate reforms that were supported by the towns but condemned by the nobility and the leading Protestant reformer, Martin Luther. Horrified by the prospect of a bloody revolution, Luther urged the rulers to crush the rebels without mercy.

4. Carefully write the rest of your essay.

Now that you have written a strong thesis, your final step is to finish your essay. As you write your essay, remember that you must address at least seven documents, analyze the point of view of at least three documents, and organize the documents into at least three appropriate groups.

Here is the rest of the sample essay for the 2008 DBQ:

> *The peasants had a number of economic grievances. Documents 2, 3, and 8 reflect their discontent.* [Note: This is the first of the three mandatory groups.] *In Twelve Articles of the Swabian Peasants (Document 2), peasant leaders complain that the lords forced them to perform services without compensation. In the Articles of the Peasants of Memmingen (Document 3), the peasants accuse the nobles of turning them into serfs. Since they were written by peasant leaders, it is reasonable to assume that Documents 2 and 3 represent widely held peasant views.* [Note: This is an example of using two documents to discuss a collective point of view. Keep in mind that it counts for only one of your three required point-of-view interpretations.] *The peasants had reason to feel exploited. In fact, they were forced to pay feudal dues, church tithes, and state taxes while the nobles and clergy were exempt from taxation. The peasants also resented the merchants growing wealth. Lorenz Fries stresses this anger in his secret report to the Archbishop of Wurzburg (Document 8). Because Fries's report is secret, it most likely states his candid opinions.* [Note: This is the second of the required point-of-view interpretations. In addition, this paragraph specifically discussed three documents.]
>
> *Protestant religious ideas also played a major role in causing the peasants' revolts. Documents 1, 3, and 6 demonstrate how the peasants used religious ideas to express and justify their demands for change.* [Note: This is the second of the three mandatory groups.] *Leonhard von Eck understood the key role of Protestant ideas when he reported to Duke Ludwig that "this rebellion ... has its ultimate source*

in Lutheran teaching" (Document 1). Although von Eck is a high government official who has a stake in preserving order and stability, his assessment is insightful. [Note: This is the third of the three required point-of-view interpretations.] *Martin Luther and other Protestant reformers had proclaimed the spiritual freedom of Christians from the Catholic Church. Peasant leaders such as Thomas Muntzer believed that "God's will" also included freedom from lords and princes (Document 6). The peasants' use of religious ideas to express their social and economic demands can be clearly seen in Document 3 in which the peasants challenge the legitimacy of serfdom by stating that "Christ purchased and redeemed us with His precious blood, just as He has the Emperor."* [Note: This paragraph specifically discusses three more documents. Just one more to go to reach the required seven!]

Responses to the peasants' revolts varied from class to class. The towns' responses (Documents 4, 5, and 9) were very different from the nobles' responses (Documents 8, 10, 11, and 12). [Note: We now have four groups, one more than required.] *The townspeople initially sympathized with the grievances of the peasants and shared their antipathy toward the nobles. In Document 9, Caspar Nutzel admits that the peasants "overstepped the mark" but reminds Duke Albert that they were provoked by the nobles' excessive greed. This sympathy translated into support when the townspeople of Weinsburg opened the town's gates so that rebellious peasants could plunder the local count's castle (Document 5). Above all, the townspeople prized peace and profit. These priorities can be clearly seen when the Memmingen Town Council (Document 4) offered to demonstrate its "good will" by freeing their serfs in exchange for payment of "a reasonable amount of money."* [Note: This paragraph specifically discusses three documents bringing the total to nine, two more than required.]

The nobles did not share the townspeople's willingness to negotiate and compromise with the peasants. Recognizing that the peasant revolt posed a direct threat to their economic and political power, the nobles condemned the uprising (Documents 1, 8, 10, 11, and 12) and took vigorous action to suppress it. The Decree of the Imperial Diet of Spey-

er (Document 12) demanded that the peasants be punished and forced to unconditionally surrender before social order could be restored. The nobles successfully used their superior military power to defeat the peasants, killing as many as 100,000 people. [Note: This paragraph discusses a tenth document and notes a fifth group.]

The nobles found an important ally in Martin Luther. Luther believed that Christians should always obey their rulers and that rebellion against the state was always wrong and must be crushed. Luther's violent response toward the peasants may have been motivated by his hatred of "that devil" Thomas Muntzer (Document 7) and his continuing dependence upon the local princes for protection from Emperor Charles V and the pope. [Note: This paragraph discusses an eleventh document and analyzes the point of view in a fifth document.]

A potent combination of economic grievances and Protestant religious ideas caused the peasants' revolts in the German states from 1524 to 1526. Social class played a key role in determining how people responded to the uprisings. Townspeople generally preferred peaceful accommodation while the nobility ultimately used their superior military power to defeat the peasants and protect their privileges. [Note: The final paragraph clearly restates the thesis.]

Strategies for the Free-Response Essays

After completing your document-based essay question (DBQ), you will yearn for a break to rest your tired writing hand. Unfortunately, there is no break. Instead, you must be resolute and focus on the next and final APEURO challenge: the free-response essays.

You will have 70 minutes to complete two free-response essays. The free-response essays are grouped into two sets. Part B of your exam contains three essay questions and Part C of your exam also contains three essay questions. The directions ask you to choose one question from Part B and one question from Part C.

Each free-response question will be scored on a scale from 1 to 9. Here are the scoring guidelines used by College Board readers:

8 to 9: Essay contains a clear, well-developed thesis supported with considerable relevant historical information.

5 to 7: Essay contains a partially developed thesis supported with some relevant historical information.

2 to 4: Essay contains a confused and unfocused thesis supported with few relevant facts.

0 to 1: Essay lacks a thesis and demonstrates little or no understanding of the question.

Each point on the 1-to-9 scale is worth 2.75 exam points. So a perfect score of 9 is worth 24.75 points, a 6 is worth 16.50 points, and a 4 is worth 11 points. The two free-response essays are worth a combined total of 49.50 points. It is important to keep in mind that a 6 will keep you on pace to earn an overall score of 5 on the APEURO exam.

Practice is the key to performing well on the free-response essays. Although practice will not guarantee a perfect score, it will help you earn a high score. The *2009 AP European History Released Exam* and the *2004 AP European History Released Exam* both include actual free-response questions and scored sample essays. Both booklets can be purchased from the College Board's online store. In addition, you should visit the AP European History Course Homepage at AP Central (*www.apcentral.collegeboard.com*). You will find a full set of free-response questions and sample essays from 1999 to the present.

STRATEGIES FOR SUCCESS

Using authentic practice materials is important. Following good strategies is essential. This section will discuss five strategies that will help you achieve high scores on your free-response essays:

1. **Make pragmatic choices.**

   Your first task is to select which of the three questions in Part B and Part C you want to write on. Above all, make a pragmatic or practical choice. Use the five-minute planning period before each part to carefully evaluate the three questions. Always choose the question that you know the most about.

2. **Make studying the Cold War a priority.**

   Many APEURO courses do not reach the Cold War period (1945–1991). As a result, many students believe that the test writers will not include an essay on post–World War II history. This view is totally wrong. Of the 108 free-response questions asked since the 2000 exam, 11 have focused on the Cold War period. There has been a Cold War–era question on either the A or B version of the APEURO exam each year for the last decade. You can use this predictable and consistent record to your advantage. Make sure that you read the Cold War chapters in your APEURO textbook. Then study Chapter 22, "The Cold War and Beyond," in this book. It provides a concise digest of the key information you will need to know about the Cold War era.

3. **Make studying women's history a priority.**

    Women's history will be a key component of your APEURO exam. Of the 108 free-response questions asked since the 2000 exam, 11 have focused on an aspect of women's history. There has been a women's history free-response question on either the A or B version of the APEURO exam 9 of the 10 years since 2000. (The 2001 exam was the only year without a woman's history free-response question.) You can use this predictable and consistent pattern to your advantage. Make sure that you read the relevant sections on women's history in your APEURO textbook. Then study Chapter 25, "Key Events, Trends, and Figures in European Women's History," in this book. It provides a carefully researched list of the key facts about women's history from the Renaissance to the present.

4. **Write a clear, well-developed thesis.**

    Remember, a thesis statement is your position on the question. Writing a clear, well-developed thesis statement is essential to earning a high score. Make sure that your thesis fully addresses the entire question. For example, the 2004 B exam included the following free-response question:

    To what extent did Romanticism challenge Enlightened views of human beings and the natural world?

    Here is a clear and fully developed thesis statement for this question:

    > *Romanticism represented a direct challenge to the Enlightenment's views of human beings and the natural world. Led by the philosophes, Enlightened thinkers believed that human beings are guided by reason and that the natural world is a vast mechanism whose secrets can be discovered by reason and formulated into natural laws. In contrast, Romanticists protested against the Enlightenment's excessive reliance on reason. Romantic poets and artists believed that human beings are driven by powerful and often irrational emotions. They looked to the natural world as a mysterious force that should be contemplated with awe and reverence. The two movements' very different views of nature and the natural world can be seen in their impact upon religion.*

5. **Write a fully developed essay.**

Now that you have written your thesis, your final step is to write a well-organized and fully developed essay. Here is the rest of the sample essay:

The Enlightenment rested on a strong belief in the ability of reason to understand human nature. Enlightened writers such as Voltaire and Diderot hated ignorance and intolerance. They believed that reason was the alternative to superstition and prejudice. In contrast, Romantics stressed the primacy of the heart over the head. Romantics preferred to rely on intuition and subjective feelings. While the philosophes valued order and natural laws, the Romantics valued spontaneous feelings. Romantic artists depicted states of mind for the first time in Western art. They portrayed insanity, dreams, and nightmares. This emphasis upon states of mind anticipated Freud's work on the subconscious.

The Scientific Revolution and the work of Newton had a strong influence on how Enlightened thinkers viewed the natural world. The philosophes believed that natural laws regulated both the universe and human society. While the philosophes investigated the natural world, Romantic artists chose to depict the natural world as a mysterious force best viewed with awe. For example, the German artist Caspar David Friedrich captured the essence of the Romantic view of the natural world in his painting, "Wanderer Looking Over a Sea of Fog." Friedrich's solitary "wanderer" stands alone on a rocky cliff pondering a landscape shrouded in thick mists.

The Enlightened and Romantic views of human nature and the natural world affected religious thought in very different ways. Enlightened thinkers rejected faith and favored the Deist view that a distant God created the natural world and like a "divine watchmaker" stepped back and let it run according to natural laws. In contrast, Romantics embraced the wonder and mysteries of nature as a way to feel the divine presence.

This stress on emotions, inner faith, and religious inspiration can be seen in the nineteenth-century religious revivals and the growing popularity of Pietism and Methodism.

The Romantic movement represented a repudiation of the Enlightenment's view of human nature and the natural world. Romantic authors and artists rejected reason and emphasized emotion. This new emphasis upon feeling and intuition led to the first attempts to probe the unconscious and to a widespread religious revival.